# ESSENTIALS OF THE FAITH

Proceeds from the sale of this book go to missions

## CITIPOINTE CHURCH
LINKED TOGETHER TO IMPACT THE WORLD

# ESSENTIALS OF THE FAITH

# Book 1: Foundations

Gary L. Taylor

Copyright © 2005, 2022 Gary L. Taylor

All rights reserved. No part of this publication may be reproduced, distributed, or transmitted in any form or by any means, including photocopying, recording, or other electronic or mechanical methods, without the prior written permission of the publisher, except in the case of brief quotations embodied in critical reviews and certain other non-commercial uses permitted by copyright law.

Unless otherwise noted, all scriptures quoted are from the NEW KING JAMES VERSION®. Copyright© 1982 by Thomas Nelson, Inc. Used by permission. All rights reserved

Scripture quotations marked "AMP" are taken from the Amplified® Bible, Copyright © 1954, 1958, 1962, 1964, 1965, 1987 by The Lockman Foundation. Used by permission.

Scripture quotations marked (NIV) are taken from the Holy Bible, New International Version®, NIV®. Copyright © 1973, 1978, 1984 by Biblica, Inc.™Used by permission of Zondervan. All rights reserved worldwide.

Scripture quotations marked (NLT) are taken from the Holy Bible, New Living Translation, copyright © 1996, 2004, 2007 by Tyndale House Foundation. Used by permission of Tyndale House Publishers, Inc., Carol Stream, Illinois 60188. All rights reserved.

Essentials of the Faith: Book 1: Foundations/ Gary L. Taylor
ISBN: 978-1-959952-00-8

# DEDICATION

To my wife, Delores, who has been my faithful companion in the many twists and turns of decades of ministry.  To all the partners of Citipointe Church upon whom these revelations were honed.

*Come to Me, all you who labor and are heavy laden, and I will give you rest. Take My yoke upon you and learn from Me, for I am gentle and lowly in heart, and you will find rest for your souls. For My yoke is easy and My burden is light.*
—Jesus

# CONTENTS

**LIFE** ...................................................................................................1
    THE VITAL PRINCIPLE ..........................................................2
    AUTHORITY ..............................................................................3
    LANGUAGE ...............................................................................3
    ABUNDANCE ............................................................................4
    PURITY ........................................................................................5
    LOVE ............................................................................................6

**SIN** .....................................................................................................11
    CREATED IN THE IMAGE OF GOD ....................................12
    SO EXACTLY WHAT IS SIN? ................................................16
    SIN AND THE OLD TESTAMENT .......................................16
    SIN AND THE NEW TESTAMENT ......................................20
    SIN AND THE WORLD ..........................................................23
    SIN AND THE BELIEVER .....................................................27

**REPENTANCE** .................................................................................33
    WHAT REPENTANCE IS NOT! .............................................33
    SO WHAT IS REPENTANCE? ...............................................37
    THREE GREEK WORDS ........................................................38
    A CHANGE OF PURPOSE ....................................................39
    GODLY REPENTANCE IS NECESSARY FOR SALVATION ..........43
    REPENTANCE AND GRACE ................................................44
    HOW DOES THIS TYPE OF REPENTANCE OCCUR? .....48
    TRANSFORMED THINKING ................................................49
    SOME AREAS OF REPENTANCE FOR BELIEVERS .......50

## MERCY ........................................................................55
### THE GREAT PARADOX .......................................................56
### MERCY IN THE OLD TESTAMENT ......................................62
### MERCY IN THE NEW TESTAMENT .....................................66

## GRACE .........................................................................73
### SO, WHAT IS GRACE? .........................................................75
### GRACE GIVES US MERIT ....................................................80
### HIS GRACE PROVIDES FAVOR ...........................................82
### HOW DO WE ACCESS THIS GREAT GRACE? ....................86

## EMPOWERMENT ........................................................ 89
### JUSTIFICATION ...................................................................90
#### JUSTIFICATION AND GRACE ...................................................91
#### JUSTIFICATION AND FAITH .....................................................93
### SANCTIFICATION ................................................................96
#### GOD'S ROLE IN SANCTIFICATION ...........................................98
#### MAN'S ROLE IN SANCTIFICATION .........................................99
### GLORIFICATION ................................................................102

# INTRODUCTION

God created man with divine intent to fulfill a divine purpose. *Essentials of the Faith* leads the reader on a path of discovery of the essential truths of that divine intent. The six-book series creates a solid, systematic understanding of who we are in Christ and how to live out that divine purpose.

### *BOOK 1: FOUNDATIONS*
The concept of the vital principle of life is explored. Its creation by God, loss by man and restoration by grace are examined.

### *BOOK 2: COVENANTS*
The restoration of divine intent is based upon our covenant relationship with God. God's covenants with man are probed and their benefits, conditions and costs are revealed.

### *BOOK 3: RELATIONSHIPS*
Love demands expression and God is love. Discover how we were created as recipients of that expression. As recipients, we become carriers of that expression.

### *BOOK 4: BLESSINGS*
Christ is the Anointed One and we are His followers. Examine the truth that as Christians we are disciples of the Anointing. As such, we are blessed and carry a blessing.

### *BOOK 5: FAITH*
The Scriptures are clear that without faith it is impossible to please God. Put your faith on solid ground as you learn the principles and power of faith.

### *BOOK 6: CHURCH LIFE*
No Christian is an island. We are all part of the body of Christ and that body has organization, power and life. Discover how each part fits together to fulfill God's divine intent.

# CHAPTER 1

# LIFE

*I have come that they may have life and that they may have it more abundantly. "I am the good shepherd. The good shepherd gives His life for the sheep"*
Jesus

*Life* was one of America's most popular magazines during the middle half of the 20th century. Its quality photos printed on oversized (11"x14"), glossy paper brought the news to life. It became a staple for millions of American coffee tables in the 1960's. For thirty-five cents, a person could see pictures from around the world and get a quick glimpse of the week's news events.

During this period, a primary school teacher devised some thought-provoking questions for her class. Her plan was to use these questions as essay topics for her young scholars. She addressed her first question to a young man who was extremely intelligent, but most often used that intellect for childish humor.

"Johnny, what is life?" she asked.

Without a moment's hesitation, Johnny replied, "Life is a magazine, Mrs. Grant."

Trying to salvage the topic, Mrs. Grant asked, "So how much is Life worth, Johnny?"

"Well, I don't rightly know how much its worth, Mrs. Grant. But it costs thirty-five cents," Johnny thoughtfully answered.

"But I only have twenty-five cents," Mrs. Grant appealed.

"That's life!" came the glib response.

This little parody speaks volumes about how many people think about life. It is as though life is something to be endured rather than a journey to be enjoyed. People act like life is out to get them: that life is trying to steal from them or bring bad things upon them. When things go wrong you will often hear people say, "Well, that's life." But is that all there is to life . . . a mere existence? Is that the way it is supposed to be?

From the earliest times man has tried to understand and explain the essence and meaning of life. Greek philosophers of old speculated as to whether what we experience is really life or if it is merely the shadow of life in another reality. In more recent days we hear new postulates on life like Rene Descartes, "I think, therefore, I am." But in all our thinking, have we really come to an understanding of life? And in all our attempts to "live life" big are we really "living" any better?

As you read the first two chapters of the Bible, you find God creating all the living creatures in the sea and the birds in the air. He then commanded the earth to "bring forth the living creature according to its kind: cattle and creeping thing and beast of the earth, each according to its kind." All these creatures are said to be "living." When God created man, He created him as a "living being."

So, what is the difference between man and the rest of the living creatures God created? Many today feel that there is no real difference. Much of biology refers to man as just another creature: just a highly evolved mammal. Are we just the highest mammal? Is there any real difference between us and animals?

## THE VITAL PRINCIPLE

According to Genesis 2:7, the Lord breathed into Adam's nostrils "the breath of life; and man became a living being." This life that was breathed into man is often referred to as the vital principle or the principle of life. This means that man's life sources are dependent upon the "quickening" or vitalizing power of God. As the Spirit of God flows into man, His life energies produce life in man. Man's life energies are the outflow of the life energies of

God's own being. In Psalm 36:9 the Psalmist speaks of this flow of life forces when he says, "With you is the fountain of life."

Man was created in the very image of God. That is to say, man was created with God's vital principle working in him. This means that man was created with the life of God in him. For man to fully experience life, he must walk in his original intent – that is, in the fullness of this vital principle.

## AUTHORITY

Our God is a god of absolute authority. As part of this vital principle flowing into man, man was given AUTHORITY. In the Creation Story, God gives man dominion over all the earth and all the living things on the earth. He gave man authority to rule this planet. Adam's first act of authority was giving names to all the animals. Genesis 2:19-20 tells the story of God bringing the animals to Adam, "whatever Adam called each living creature, that was its name. So Adam gave names to all cattle, to the birds of the air and to every beast of the field."

Just a few generations later, mankind had become so evil that God was sorry that He ever created man. He determined to start afresh with Noah and his family. After the flood, God blessed Noah and his sons. He gave them the same command that he gave Adam – to be fruitful and multiply, to fill the earth and subdue it. He tells Noah that he has placed everything under his authority. Years later, King David is pondering this aspect of the vital principle and he writes, "You have crowned man with glory and honor. You made him to have dominion over the works of Your hands" (Psalm 8:5).

## LANGUAGE

Another characteristic of this vital principle is LANGUAGE. Because of the authority given to man, language was a necessary attribute of man. Authority is expressed through language. God and His word are inseparable. In John 1:1, John reveals, "In the beginning was the Word and the Word was with God and the Word was God." Through His Word, He created everything that was created. He spoke into the vast emptiness of nothingness and that which did not exist took on existence.

When He created man in His own image, God gave him complex language skills that enabled man to express his authority and communicate his thoughts very clearly. This communication skill was so thorough that in only a few short years man had come to the place that nothing could stop him. Eleven chapters into the Bible, we find the story of the tower of Babel. Language united the people and they aspired to reach the heavens by their own strength. To thwart their plans, God confused their unified language. They could no longer communicate with one another. Their grand plans came to an abrupt end. The wise sage Solomon gave expression to the power of language when he wrote, "Death and life are in the power of the tongue" (Proverbs 18:21).

## ABUNDANCE

The God Who Is dwells in abundance. The Scriptures teach that nothing is too difficult for Him. He paves His streets with gold. His gates are constructed of pearl, and precious jewels are the building material for His walls. In verse 5 of that most famous of Psalms, Psalm 23, David says that when God prepares a meal for us our cups run over. And in another place, he writes, "Every beast of the forest is mine and the cattle on a thousand hills . . . for the world is mine and all its fullness" (Psalm 50:10,12).

ABUNDANCE is a part of God's character and as such, is another part of this vital principle that was breathed into man. Man was created for abundance. The Garden of Eden was a place of abundance. It was the perfect ecological system for it came forth from the mind of the Creator. In the Garden, there was abundance. Everything man needed was provided in abundance. David eloquently portrayed this abundance in Psalm 23. "The Lord is my shepherd; I shall not want." There is no want in abundance.

Abundance is the state of possessing more than enough. When we think of the abundance of God, that abundance goes beyond simply having more than enough. Even His abundance is in abundance. His abundance is infinite. All the attributes of

God speak of His infinite nature. He is omnipotent. His power is infinite. It knows no limits. His knowledge and wisdom are infinite. He is omniscient. Our God knows no limits in any area. He is a God of infinite abundance.

This principle of extreme abundance is precisely what Paul was referring to in 1 Corinthians 2 when he wrote that eye has not seen, nor the ear heard, nor even been imaged, the good things God has stored up for us. He expresses the infinite nature of God's abundance in Ephesians 3:20. "Now to Him who is able to do exceedingly abundantly above all that we ask or think, according to the power that works in us." God's abundance is so excessive that our finite minds cannot even grasp it.

Because this infinite abundance is an attribute of God, this abundance was breathed into man as part of the vital principle of life. Man was created for a life of abundance. It is no wonder that man in his present state is never satisfied and is always seeking more. Nelson Rockefeller, with all his vast fortune, was once asked how much it would take to satisfy him. Mr. Rockefeller replied, "Just a little bit more." The life force in man cries out for an abundance of all things for God is a God of abundance.

## PURITY

Yet another aspect of this vital principle we receive from God's character is PURITY. No one enjoys life more than an innocent child. There is a perfect bliss in naiveté. Oh, how much we lose when we lose our innocence. Until we learn to know the pain and ugliness of evil, we live life on an entirely different level. That is the level of life that God breathed into man. No impurity can dwell in His presence. For this reason, Hebrews 12:29 says that our "God is a consuming fire." His very presence consumes all impurity, His habitation is a place of perfect purity. When His Number One angel, Lucifer, allowed impurity into his being, he was removed from heaven.

The purity of life in God's presence is without compromise. For only in purity can one truly know the God kind of life. John, the apostle, tells us in 1 John 3 that as Jesus reveals Himself to us, we become like Him. Revelation builds upon revelation, and we begin to see Him as He is (the King of Kings and Lord of Lords). As we begin to see Him as He is, we begin to conform to His image. Those who walk in this revelation, purify themselves even as He is pure. This desire for purity is part of the vital principle breathed into man.

## LOVE

But above all else, the greatest vital principle that overflowed from God's being into man is LOVE. God doesn't just possess love, "God is love" (1 John 4:16). God created man in His own image to have relationship with him for by its very nature, love demands release and expression.

Man was created as recipient of God's very essence – His love. In order for man to fully participate in this love relationship, he had to be made love as well. Because God breathed His very essence into man – man loves. In the lives of the most hardened criminals, we find acts of paradoxical love. This is because this vital principle was placed in man by God and man cannot fully escape it. According to 1 Corinthians 13:13, love is the greatest of all the forces that flow through us.

But rather than embrace and simply enjoy the God given life forces, man chose knowledge over life. There were two main trees in the Garden of Eden. The Tree of Life and the Tree of Knowledge of Good and Evil. The Lord told man that he could eat of all that was in the garden. Man was free to eat of the Tree of Life, whenever he chose.

There was only one exception to this liberty; man was forbidden to eat of the Tree of Knowledge of Good and Evil. God's word was that if he ate of that tree he would die. The moment he ate of that tree he would die to the TRUE LIFE God meant for him to experience. The moment he chose the Tree of Knowledge, he lost the vital principle of life.

The moment man ate of that tree, he ceased to be like God. In the Garden, the serpent told Eve that she would become like God if she ate of the forbidden fruit. Nothing could have been further from the truth. God's vital principle had been breathed into her. She was already like God. In that likeness, there is only good.

God does not know evil. He is totally good. He is familiar with evil and understands its consequences. But He does not know evil personally. His glory is His goodness.

Created in the very image of God, man had no knowledge of evil. But the moment he ate of that fruit, he no longer retained the likeness of God. He now knew evil. He was now like the serpent, knowing good and evil. With that knowledge came the loss of innocence. Man no longer lived in the bliss of purity. His choice caused the forfeiture of the absolute joy of absolute goodness. But man could not resist the allurement of evil and he ate of the forbidden, costly fruit. With that defiant act, he lost the life he was created to enjoy.

From that moment until now, man has been on a quest to regain that life he was created to enjoy. Man has followed many avenues thinking he would find that life. Drugs, money, alcohol, sex, power . . . all are part of man's futile quest to find life as it should be. But all these avenues are dead ends. Solomon in all his wisdom clarified the futility of this quest when he wrote, "There is a way that seems right to a man, but its end is the way of death" (Proverbs 16:25). Man goes out looking for life but only finds death. Despite all of his attempts, he cannot restore the vital principle.

Jesus came to provide the only avenue back into this original intent of man's creation. It is for this reason that He said, "I am the way, the truth and the life. No one comes to the Father except through me" (John 14:6). Only through Christ is the vital principle restored. Jesus came as God incarnate – that is, God in the flesh. As God in the flesh, Jesus was also LIFE in the flesh. In his gospel account, John puts it this way – "In Him (Jesus) was life and the life was the light of men" (John 1:4).

That which God breathed into man in the garden, Jesus brings into man with His indwelling. He is life personified. If He dwells in us and we dwell in Him, life indwell us. His desire is that we experience this life we were created to enjoy. Jesus Himself said, "I have come that they may have life and they may have it more abundantly" (Joh 10:10). Jesus did not come to give man mere existence. He came to restore the vital principle of life.

In Luke 19:10, Jesus says that He came to "seek and save that which was lost." The word that is translated "save" literally means to restore or make whole. Notice that He came to restore "that" which was lost. What was lost? LIFE. By His death and resurrection, Jesus restored the vital principle to man. That truth is beautifully explained in Ephesians 2:4-7. "But God, who is rich in mercy, because of His great love with which He loved us, even when we were dead in trespasses, made us alive together with Christ (by grace you have been saved) and raised us up together and made us sit together in the heavenly places in Christ Jesus, that in the ages to come He might show the exceeding riches of His grace in His kindness toward us in Christ Jesus." In Christ, the vital principle is restored. God's image is restored in us. What was lost in Adam is restored in Christ. We are made alive once again. We are restored to our position of relationship with the Father.

For this reason, Romans 6:4 tells us that we are to "walk in the newness of life." Jesus restores the vital principle back to man. As Christians, we have the life of God dwelling in us. We are not just going to exist forever – we are going to have God-life forever. According to John 17:3, eternal life is "knowing God." That which was lost in the garden is restored in Jesus. That is why Paul says in Galatians 2:20, "I have been crucified with Christ; it is no longer I who live, but Christ lives in me; and the life which I now live in the flesh I live by faith in the Son of God, who loved me and gave Himself for me."

As followers of Christ, we are ambassadors of this life. The words of Paul in 2 Corinthians 5 stand as a mission statement to all believers. "Therefore, if anyone is in Christ, he is a new creation; old things have passed away; behold, all things have become new. (*The death-life of mere existence is finished and the fullness of life has come*). Now all things are of God, who has reconciled us to Himself through Jesus Christ and has given us the ministry of reconciliation, that is, that God was in Christ reconciling the world to Himself, not imputing their trespasses to them and has committed to us the word of reconciliation. Now then, we are ambassadors for Christ, as though God were pleading through us: we implore you on Christ's behalf, be reconciled to God." Christ came to reconcile us to God; to restore the vital principle of life to us. In Christ, we are new creations, walking in the newness of life.

If you are not walking in this newness of life that Christ promised, what are you waiting for? Today is the day to be restored to that fullness of life – that vital principle of God.

# CHAPTER 2

# SIN

*But your iniquities have separated you from your God;*
*And your sins have hidden His face from you,*
*So that He will not hear*
Isaiah 59:2

In our 21st century world of selfish, self-indulgent, situational ethics, there seems to be no room for the concept of sin. People "make mistakes" or have a problem but none dare use the word "sin". Guilt has become a bad word. Yet, guilt is a symptom of sin in our psyche much like pain is a symptom of injury or disease in our physical body. Guilt makes us uncomfortable with ourselves.

In his classic book, *Crime and Punishment*, Russian author, Fyodor Dostoevsky, wrote of the powerful effects guilt can have upon a human. The lead character, Raskolnikov, commits the perfect crime only to be driven mad by his own guilt. Rewritten today, we would have to entitle it something like Making a Mistake But Failing To Get Away With It.

Our world tries to eliminate guilt by using phraseology void of moral content. After all, how can we be held guilty of something that is really a disease of addiction (sex addiction, drug addiction, alcoholism, etc.) or social upbringing? If it is wrong, it is not our fault; it is the way we were raised. Modern psychology has become proficient at casting the moral blame on others to explain away our own moral ineptitudes.

But the concept of sin was not instantaneously eradicated from our vocabulary by pushing some cosmic delete button. It has been fading into the sunset for the past few decades. Back in 1973, American psychologist Karl Menninger observed that the word "sin" was rarely heard. In his book, *Whateve Became of Sin?*, Menninger noted:

> "Does that mean that no sin is involved in all our troubles — sin with an 'I' in the middle? Is no one any longer guilty of anything? Guilty perhaps of a sin that could be repented and repaired or atoned for? Is it only that someone may be stupid or sick or criminal — or asleep? Wrong things are being done, we know; tares are being sown in the wheat field at night. But is no one responsible, no one answerable for these acts?"[1]

Menninger speaks of the "disappearance of sin" and the "the twilight of sin". The thought and vocabulary of modern man has no place for sin -- at least in Western societies. Repentance is unnecessary and unreasonable when the act is not one's fault. Just apologize for the mistake or weakness. It seems that the word sin has become distasteful to modern man and he has discarded it. No matter what we call it, sin is still sin and still carries all of its awful consequences.

William Shakespeare understood this fact when he penned those famous words of Lady Macbeth, "Out! Out damned spot! Out, I say." This spot she refers to is not some coffee or tea stain. It is the guilt of sin. She and her husband killed King Duncan. Now, they wrestle with the psychological symptoms of that sin. Macbeth himself says that all the water in the ocean could not wash his hands of Duncan's blood. Sin along with its consequences and remedy is one of the main themes of the Bible.

## CREATED IN THE IMAGE OF GOD

When God created man, he created him as a free moral agent. In the Garden of Eden everything man needed could be found. It was there at his disposal. The only exception was the Tree of

---

[1] Karl A. Menninger,*Whatever Became of Sin?* (New York: Hawthorn Books, 1993)

Knowledge of Good and Evil. God strictly forbade man to eat of this tree. "Of every tree of the garden you may freely eat; but of the tree of the knowledge of good and evil you shall not eat, for in the day that you eat of it you shall surely die" (Genesis 2:16-17).

But God could not actually stop these original humans from disobeying – even though it brought corruption to His creation. As a free moral agent, man had to be permitted choice, even if he made the wrong choice. If man was to have relationship with God, the creator of the universe, he had to be a ruler himself – man had to be able to choose for himself. He had to be able to control his own life.

Adam and Eve dwelt in divine perfection. Up until this point, man knew only good. There was no evil. In my version, mosquitoes did not bite. Fire ants had no fire. Everything was in submission to them. All creation was under man's dominion. Humans ruled everything. Even the insects obeyed them. For man to have deep relationship with God, he had to understand what it was like to have authority. God has absolute authority. Power and authority carry heavy responsibility. How could man possibly relate to Him if he did not personally understand authority and power? Man had full authority upon the earth. Man was given authority and choice. But man made the wrong choice. He ate of the wrong tree. Adam ate of the tree of good and evil.

At its very root, sin is simply unbelief. Sin says, "I know more about what is good for me than God does." The "Thou Shalt Nots" of the Bible are not given to prohibit us from enjoying life; they are there to keep us out of death. When God says that man is to work six days and rest one, He was not trying to keep us from enjoying life. He is the maker of the body and He said, "You need one day to rejuvenate your life sources." If you have ever had to work seven days a week for periods of time, you find that your production goes down. You are working more hours, but you are not producing more. You were not designed to keep that kind of schedule. You were designed to have a day of rest. You need that day to recover, recuperate and restore your resources. He did not tell us to only work six days to punish us. He gave us His laws so that we could have life. When we violate those laws, we are saying to God, "I know more about what is good for me than You do."

Up to the time that man chose to disobey this command of God, he knew only good. But when he ate of that tree, he opened the door for the entrance of evil into all mankind. When Adam sinned, he opened up a floodgate of evil into all of us. The penalty was not simply death for himself; it was death for all of mankind. We lost relationship with God and life. Everything was changed; nothing was the same as it had been before the fall. Not only did Adam and Eve die to perfect goodness, all mankind also died. In Paul's letter to the church at Rome, he makes the issue clear, "For as by one man's disobedience many were made sinners" (Romans 5:19). By that one act, sin entered into the human race and we all became sinners. We do not sin and therefore, become sinners. We are sinners by nature – sinners by heritage and birth – therefore, we sin. The act of sin is simply the fulfillment of that sinful nature.

Therefore, Adam's act of disobedience was more than just an action. The real issue is the heart that motivated the act. Disobedience is actually an act of unbelief that refuses to acknowledge the truth that God knows what is best for us. This sinful act in the Garden quickly developed into an evil disposition so widespread that God had to respond. "Then the LORD saw that the wickedness of man was great in the earth and that every intent of the thoughts of his heart was only evil continually. And the LORD was sorry that He had made man on the earth and He was grieved in His heart. So the LORD said, 'I will destroy man whom I have created from the face of the earth, both man and beast, creeping thing and birds of the air, for I am sorry that I made them" (Genesis 6:5-7). Man's sinful disposition had polluted the whole earth.

This statement, "I am sorry that I have made them" is disturbing to us. Did God not know what was going to happen to us when he made us? It seems that the one thing God did not know about was sin. He did not know what sin was going to do to man. He did not know all the ramifications. God did not know sin. God cannot know sin. God is God. In Him is only goodness. God cannot understand rebellion in a personal way. It is incongruous to His goodness. Just before His crucifixion, Jesus was praying in the Garden of Gethsemane. As He thought on the idea of taking the sin of the world in His body, He prayed, "Father, if there is any other way, let this cup pass from me." He was not afraid of the nails, the scourging, or the dying. He knew He would live again. He was spirit. He had existed before that time and would exist after that time. His concern was that He was about to take on sin. He knew absolutely nothing of sin in His person. He did not know sin. He had no personal experiential knowledge of sin.

Let me illustrate this with a concept from the Old Testament. When the Scriptures are explaining the sexual relationship between a man and wife, it uses the word "knew." Abraham "knew" Sarah. That word is used to explain that in his deepest place, he had intimate, personal knowledge, and relationship with his wife. In the New Testament, Paul says, "He made Him who knew no sin to be sin for us" (2 Corinthians 5:21). Jesus had no intimate, experiential understanding of sin.

According to Scripture, everything that was created was created by the Word; created by Jesus. But God did not create sin. God did not create rebellion. Man, in his infinite wisdom, chose to listen to the serpent's lies. He chose to unbelieve. God created the choice to believe, and man chose not to believe. God had to give man an option to provide the choice of free agency. Without another option, there is no choice. But God not only gave the option, He gave instruction with the option. He told man what to do: "Don't eat of that tree." God created the choice, but man created sin.

In the days of Noah, God came to the place where He said, "I am sorry that I made man." At that point God destroyed the earth with the flood and started all over with Noah. But things were not that much better with Noah's lineage. Almost immediately after getting off the ark, Noah gets drunk. We are not sure exactly what happened when he got drunk, but it was not a good thing. Sin still abounded. The sinful heart was still there. Sin had entered into the spiritual DNA of man. Man was a sinner by nature. That is why the Law cannot eradicate sin, it can only act as a control mechanism.

## SO EXACTLY WHAT IS SIN?

According to the Bible, anything that is "not of faith is sin" (Romans 14:23). Sin is the failure to believe that God knows what is best and that what He is telling you is in your own best interest. Sin can be defined as "transgressing the law," and that transgression is lawlessness. That is, sin is determining not to be ruled by law. Sin is the refusal to submit to God's authority as expressed through His law. Scripture says, "Whoever commits sin also commits lawlessness and sin is lawlessness" (1 John 3:4). Refusal to submit to what God says is unbelief. If we really believe God loves us and wants what is best for us, we will do what He tells us to do. We enter into lawlessness because we do not trust God. It is a heart condition, a matter of the will. This heart condition creates desires and desires create actions. In its most common usage, sin is an act. But it comes from the heart and then changes the person who commits the act.

Sin would be a simple thing if it could be kept outside. As surely as Adam and Eve sinned when they ate of that tree of knowledge of good and evil, we partake of that same knowledge of evil when we sin. Once we have partaken of that knowledge of evil, we are never the same. We are changed in our innermost qualities by that act.

## SIN AND THE OLD TESTAMENT

The Hebrew word *hatta* is the most often used word for sin in the Old Testament. It is used over 150 times in its various forms. The simplest meaning of the word would be to miss the road or miss the mark. If you are traveling in a new land, you are usually limited to the use of a map to find your way. If you miss a turn, it is very easy to get lost. We say that people who do not know Jesus are lost. They have missed the road. They are still in sin. They have missed the road or missed the mark.

The word iniquity is another Old Testament word that describes sin. Iniquity is the Hebrew word *awen*. It speaks of the absence of all that has true worth. It denotes "moral worthlessness." This word's counterpart, *awon* means "to be crooked, twisted, or perverted." These words speak of sin as a perversion of life; a twisting out of the right way; a perversion of truth; a twisting into error and a perversion of intent; a twisting of freedom into willful disobedience. Iniquity is not simply a missing of the road. It is the willful choice to pervert the path.

Freedom was not given to provide us opportunity to sin. Freedom was given to enable us to show ourselves faithful and not sin. God did not give us freedom to enable us to live in sin. He created us in His image and that image involves freedom of choice. With our freedom, we were free to prove our faithfulness to the relationship with God. However, we did not use our freedom in its intended purpose. We perverted it. We twisted it. In our freedom, we missed the road of righteousness.

In the Old Testament, the prophet Isaiah speaks of the devastating effects this twisting and perverting has upon man. Isaiah says that when we sin, it creates a barrier between us and God. Sin separated man from God, because man took the wrong road or at least missed the true road. We have taken a road that leads away from God. The prophet, Isaiah, makes this fact very clear in Isaiah 59. "Behold, the LORD'S hand is not shortened, that it cannot save; nor His ear heavy, that it cannot hear. But your iniquities have separated you from your God; and your sins have hidden His face from you, so that He will not hear." The true road directs man in his journey with God. When man misses the road, he finds himself separated from God. He has chosen to follow his own path, rather than the path of God. Therefore, he is separated from God.

Many times, Christians mistakenly use this verse to describe themselves and their immediate relationship with God. They think because they have sinned, God cannot, or will not, hear them. However, for those who have come to a saving knowledge of the Lord Jesus Christ, this verse is non-applicable. Jesus told us that He would never leave us or forsake us. He did not say that

He would never leave us or forsake us as long as we did not sin. That is like a father telling his son, "You can be my son and live in my house as long as you do exactly as I say. But the first time you disobey me, you are gone."

The Old Testament model is well summed up in Deuteronomy 28. In this passage the priests stood on two opposing mountains and set the options before the children of Israel. If they disobey, they are cursed. If they obey, they are blessed. In the New Covenant, our blessing is based upon the righteousness and goodness of Christ. If He is in us, then we are blessed. As a matter of fact, Ephesians 1:3 says that God has "blessed us with every spiritual blessing." That is not a future event. The verb is past tense. He has already blessed us. In Christ, our sin has been removed "as far as the east is from the west and God remembers it no more" (Psalm 103:12, Jeremiah 31:34). Jesus became a curse for us and we are blessed in Him.

But when we walk in sin, we miss the road; we pervert or twist the way. In our disobedience, we are simply walking away from the blessing. The Prodigal Son was blessed. But he just walked away from his blessing. You may close off some avenues of blessing, but God does not curse you because you do not obey Him. However, the Scriptures do tell us that the Lord disciplines those He loves. That does not mean that grandma dies, or your child gets sick. That is not the way God disciplines His children. I would not discipline my children that way and my love is imperfect – while God's love is perfect. Why would we try to put these things on God?

We often refer to discipline as if it were punishment. But there is a difference between discipline and punishment. Punishment says that you have done wrong and have to pay a penalty for that action. Discipline says that you are acting wrong and something has to be done to change your behavior. Discipline comes to modify our behavior. God is not going to punish us for our sins. He put all of that on Jesus (1 Peter 2:24). He took all your sins in His body on the cross. Jesus became our sin and He bore our punishment. There is no punishment left. However, there is discipline and training. He will correct you and lean against you to get you going in the right way. You may bump into Him as you try to choose the wrong door, but He will not forsake you. Your sin can no longer separate you from Him.

Psalm 51 is probably the most famous chapter in all of the Old Testament about sin. This is David's psalm about his sin with Bathsheba that the prophet exposed. The prophet, Nathan, came to David and told him, "King David, there is a very prosperous man who has many sheep. His neighbor only has one little lamb. One day, friends came to visit the rich man and rather than slaughtering one of his own sheep, he stole his neighbor's one single lamb. He fed his friends with his neighbor's lamb." The Scriptures tell us that David rose from his throne. You can imagine the flush in his cheeks and the anger rising. He asks Nathan, "Who is this man? I will have him put to death." Nathan pointed his finger at David and said, "You are that man." The Scripture says that David immediately repented. Psalm 51 is his psalm of repentance.

> "Have mercy upon me, O God, according to Your loving kindness; according to the multitude of Your tender mercies, blot out my transgressions. Wash me thoroughly from my iniquity and cleanse me from my sin. For I acknowledge my transgressions and my sin is always before me. Against You, You only, have I sinned and done this evil in Your sight -- that You may be found just when You speak and blameless when You judge. Behold, I was brought forth in iniquity and in sin my mother conceived me. Behold, You desire truth in the inward parts and in the hidden part You will make me to know wisdom. Purge me with hyssop and I shall be clean; wash me and I shall be whiter than snow. Make me to hear joy and gladness, that the bones You have broken may rejoice. Hide Your face from my sins and blot out all my iniquities. Create in me a clean heart, O God and renew a steadfast spirit within me. Do not cast me away from Your presence and do not take Your Holy Spirit from me. Restore to me the joy of Your

salvation and uphold me by Your generous Spirit. Then I will teach transgressors Your ways and sinners shall be converted to You. Deliver me from bloodshed, O God, the God of my salvation, and my tongue shall sing aloud of Your righteousness. O Lord, open my lips and my mouth shall show forth Your praise. For You do not desire sacrifice, or else I would give it; you do not delight in burnt offering. The sacrifices of God are a broken spirit, a broken and a contrite heart-- these, O God, You will not despise."

Now keep in mind that David was under the Old Covenant, so his repentance includes some statements that are not true for us today. Sometimes, you hear people take this statement about God desiring a broken heart and assume that he means weeping and wailing and crying out. There is an element of truth there. God does want our brokenness. He does want us to realize that we have missed the road; that we are going the wrong way. But He is not looking for emotion. He is looking for change of heart that leads to a change of action. Many times, we take this Old Testament passage and try to bring it into New Testament reality. We do not need to ask God to blot out our iniquities, He has already done that. According to Scripture, He has forgiven our sins; removing them as far as the east is from the west and remembers them no more. We do not need to ask Him to cleanse us; He has washed us in the blood of the Lamb. We do not need to ask him to create a clean heart in us. According to Ezekiel 36:26, He has given us a new heart and placed His Word in it. God has already done His part. All we must do is turn back (repent) to Him and receive what He has already completed. God is not looking for anything from you, but your love, your relationship, and your obedience.

## SIN AND THE NEW TESTAMENT

In the New Testament the most often used word for sin is the Greek word *hamartia* and it literally means the missing of the mark. But the word has a much larger meaning than this. It is used as an inward element that produces action. In Romans 6:12, the apostle Paul tells us, "What shall we say then? Shall we continue in sin that grace may abound? Certainly not! How shall we who died to sin live any longer in it?" He is not talking about an act. He is talking about an inward element or nature. We have died to this inward element of selfish interests that demands we go our own way and do our own thing. Jesus said that no man can come after Him unless he dies to self. When He talks about dying to self, He is alluding to this same principle of dying to self-interest. He is talking about dying to that inward element that says, "I know what is better for my life than God. I will do what I want and not what God says." If we are to be followers of Christ, we must die to that inner element of sin. We must follow His road and abandon our own direction.

When God gave the Law, He did not give it as a means whereby man could become righteous. On the contrary, He gave the Law to show us how strong this inner element is. "What shall we say then? Is the law sin? Certainly not! On the contrary, I would not have known sin except through the law. For I would not have known covetousness unless the law had said, 'You shall not covet.' But sin, taking opportunity by the commandment, produced in me all manner of evil desire. For apart from the law sin was dead" (Romans 7:7-8). The Law is God's holy, righteous standard. But it is not given to us as a set of rules and regulations to make us holy.

God gave us the Law to reveal to us the inward element that was operating in us, causing us to do things the wrong things. He brought the Law to show us the deceptiveness of self-righteousness. The Scripture calls the Law the plumb line or the level. Just because things look level does not mean that they are level. When you build a house, you do not build by simple eyesight. You use the level for alignment because your eyes will deceive you. Most of you have seen the trick where you attach a glass tube to an outlet of an unattached water faucet and support the tube so that it stands up vertically. You then attach a hidden water hose to the open end of the tube and open the water supply. Your eyes will make you think that you see water coming out of a faucet that is not connected to a pipe. You are deceived -- for the water is coming up the inside of the glass tube and then washing down the outside of the tube. In this way, you cannot see the tube, but you see the water apparently flowing from the unattached faucet. But your eyes deceived you.

You have probably seen the allusion that uses a sloped floor and ceiling to create the affect that a ball is rolling up-hill. It is a deception. If you were to lay a level down on the track of the ball, you would see that the ball is still rolling downhill even though it appears to be going uphill. But the level reveals the allusion. It exposes the deception. So, it is with the Law. It reveals the allusion and deception of self-righteousness.

This word *hamartia* comes from the concept of the Old Testament word we spoke of earlier. It carries that meaning of missing the road. It speaks of a thing that is twisted. It looks correct, but it is not. This word sin is used as an organized power acting through the members of the physical body. The devil wants you to sin so that you can be distracted by wrongful thinking. Satan's greatest weapon in prohibiting us from living the life God intended is to pervert our self-image. When we sin, we become sin conscious instead of Christ conscious. If you focus on what you have done wrong, you will keep doing it wrong. If you want to walk in a righteous manner, focus on who you are in Christ and how you are supposed to live in Him.

"Knowing this, that our old man was crucified with Him, that the body of sin might be done away with, that we should no longer be slaves of sin" (Romans 6:6). Your old man – that inner interest of selfishness – is a dead man. You will often hear people say, "That was just your old nature." Your old nature should be a dead nature. If it is still alive, you need to take it to the cross. When you come to Jesus, you cannot get your new nature until you trade in your old nature. If you want to keep the old nature, He is not going to give you the new nature. You cannot have two opposing natures. If you do not have the new nature, then you are not born again and have not become a child of God. When Paul says that "the body of sin might be done away with", he is saying that sin has been rendered inoperative in your life. Think about pictures you have seen of war zones. There are always pieces of equipment sitting around that are inoperative, powerless and useless. That is the picture of innate sin in your new life.

God is not willing to share you with the devil. There are no special discounts with God. To come to Christ, the old man must die. If the old man has not died, the new man has not been born. According to 2 Corinthians 5:17, the old nature must pass away in order for a new creation to be formed. All things must become new. There is no room for the old. Suppose you had an old compass with a bent needle. That needle continually drags the face of the compass and fails to yield a true north indication. You try to use it to guide your path, but you keep finding yourself going in the wrong direction. You take the compass to a repair shop and the old, bent needle is replaced with a new, true needle. The old needle has been made inoperative, so that the new needle can direct you in the right direction.

But this word sin not only speaks of the inward parts that make man do wrong, it is also used in speaking of a deed that is wrong. James 1:15 says, "Then, when desire has conceived, it gives birth to sin; and sin, when it is full-grown, brings forth death." Here the word hamartia speaks of the action that follows the wrong thinking. Once our thinking gets twisted (once our needle is bent), our desires get twisted. Once we determine that God does not know what is best for us, we begin to desire things that we think are best for us. That is exactly what happened to Eve. Once she decided that the fruit of the tree was good, her desire for it was born. Once the desire was born, her action followed.

## SIN AND THE WORLD

As we have seen, sin is universal. When Adam and Eve sinned, all mankind sinned. Ultimately, we all trace our family back down the same lineage. We all inherit the breath we breathe from Adam and Eve. The sin of these ancient ancestors caused the entire world to be born in sin. Man is not a sinner because he sins – he sins because he is a sinner. He is of His father Adam. The Adamic nature is in all mankind.

Most people do not believe that we have an evil nature. Much of psychology teaches that you are born with a "blank slate." Life experiences make you good or bad. Although that makes great psychology, it makes for poor theology. The Bible says that you were not born a blank slate; you were born a black slate. Your heart was black from the beginning. It was black with sin.

You do not have to teach a child to do evil. You can put a child in a perfect environment, and he will still sin. It is amazing. Children are evil by nature. When my daughter, Charity, was two years old, she learned that she could bite people and hurt them. I did not teach her how to bite other children. No one taught her how to bite. One day, my oldest daughter, Krisinda, was watching television. Charity came up and bit her on the back. Unless my wife was doing something behind my back and biting her, no one taught her how to bite people to hurt them. No one had to teach her. We are born sinners. Children are not taught to pull hair. They just seem to know. They innately know how to be selfish and greedy. If one child has a toy and another child wants that toy, there is going to be a fight! We have to teach our children how to share. If they were such a blank slate, how did they learn to be selfish and not share? You can have an entire room of toys, but the one the other child has is the one they desire. As soon as they grab hold, they say, "Mine!" Their hearts are evil by nature.

When parents bring their adolescents to me for counseling, the first thing I tell the parents is, "Your children will lie." If they do not believe me, then I tell them that we cannot go any further. They are deceived. We must understand that our children have evil hearts. They inherited those sinful hearts from us. Without Christ, we are reprobates bound for hell. There is no end to the evil of which are capable. Some of you are honest enough to admit it; some of you are not. Man does not sin and become a sinner. He is born a sinner. He is just acting out who he is. The Adamic nature is in all men.

That is the issue Paul is addressing when he writes, "For all have sinned and come short of the glory of God" (Romans 3:23). It does not say that we fall short of bringing God glory. It literally says that we fall short of the God glory in which He intended us to walk. We fall short of the glory of the abundant life that God intended. We fall short of His original intent. We fall short of His divine design because we are of our father Adam.

Grace, mercy and repentance are our only hope. We will never live the kind of life God intended without the grace of God. To receive His grace, we must admit that we are sinners. If we are not sinners, we do not need His grace. John addresses this issue in his first letter to the church. In 1 John 1:8-9, he writes, "If we say that we have no sin, we deceive ourselves and the truth is not in us. If we confess our sins, He is faithful and just to forgive us our sins and to cleanse us from all unrighteousness. If we say that we have not sinned, we make Him a liar and His word is not in us." Before a person can receive the grace of God, he must recognize that he needs the grace of God. The Jewish people did not see themselves as sinners. They saw themselves as children of the promise, children of Abraham. John is saying that if we recognize (confess) that we are sinners, God will forgive us.

This passage is most often used today to instruct Christians how to pray or how to "find" forgiveness. This passage has become the sacrificial altar of the New Testament. When you sin, you have to go to this altar and get the problem fixed. The Catholic Church is built upon confession. Confession is one third of their doctrine of salvation. They say that you are saved through communion, confession, and baptism. Confession comes out of this passage. But that is a distortion of the truth. He is not talking about a believer listing his sins before the Father. He is saying, "If you think you are not a sinner – if you think that you are not guilty of sin – you are deceived. If you are unwilling or unable to admit who you are and what you have done, you are a liar and nothing can be done for you. But if you will be honest and humbly admit that you are a sinner and that you have sinned, He will forgive you."

Please notice carefully what this verse says – not what you have been told it says. "If we confess our sins, He is faithful and just to forgive our sins and cleanse us of all unrighteousness."

God is faithful and just to forgive our sins – faithful and just. Jesus bore our sins on the cross. He paid our debt. Justice demands that God forgive us. The sin debt was paid over two thousand years ago. There is not some checklist in heaven and when we confess the sin God forgives us. The Bible says that once we have given our life to Christ, we are forgiven, and God no longer even remembers our sin (Hebrews 10:17). That is exactly what John says here, "He cleanses us from all unrighteousness." He is talking about your salvation experience. He can only cleanse us from ALL unrighteousness ONCE. That is what happened at salvation.

If you do not think you have sin, you do not need a Savior. People think they are okay because they live a good life. They do not understand. They do not think that their sin is that bad. The question is not whether you are worse than most people, the question is "Are you worse than God?" The comparison is not a comparison with other men. It is a comparison with God. A comparison with perfection. Unless you are perfect, you have a problem. God cannot allow anyone but perfect people to enter heaven. Heaven is a place of perfection. To allow entrance of any imperfection would ruin the perfection. Luckily, we were allowed to trade our imperfect life for His perfect one. He became sin so that we could "become the righteousness of God in Christ Jesus" (2 Corinthians 5:21). He took our sin and gave us His righteousness. He took our old man and we received His new man. He has cleansed us from all our sin. But we cannot be cleansed if we are not willing to admit that we have sinned. This admission comes at salvation when we confess our need for a Savior.

He is talking about salvation in verse 10 of this passage in 1 John. If you have never sinned, you are not human. If you have never sinned, you do not need a savior. This was a real problem among the Jews of this period. Remember, the rich young ruler who came to Christ? He asked Jesus what he needed to do to go to heaven. Jesus told him to keep the Law. He replied that he had kept the Law from childhood. What is he claiming? He is claiming that he has never sinned. This is the very issue John is addressing. In verse 9, he tells us that if we will come to God as sinners, He will forgive us of our sin and cleanse us of all unrighteousness. That is how we come to Christ. That is how we are born again. That is how we become a follower of Christ. We admit our need and turn to Him for deliverance. But if you have never sinned, you do not need a savior. If you say you have never sinned, you make God a liar because He said that all have sinned and come short of His glory.

## SIN AND THE BELIEVER

Sin has no place in the believer's life. People tell me that I preach grace too much and give people a reason to sin. Grace does not permit you to sin; it keeps you from sinning. Grace tells you that you are the righteousness of God in Christ Jesus. As children of God, we must come to an understanding of what grace has made us and then live out that understanding. Most of us were told all our life that we were saved by grace, but we were still just dirty rotten sinners. We are getting into heaven by the skin of our teeth. As a young man I noticed that every time an evangelist came into town for revival meetings, people got re-saved. People got re-saved in the Baptist church and the Baptist church does not even believe in getting re-saved! We believed "once saved, always saved." But let a good evangelist come to town and you will find people getting saved again.

When we become convinced and convicted of our sin and sinfulness, we believe we need a Savior again. But Christ cannot die again. He took all our sin in His body on that tree. There is no sin left for Him to take. Remember, sin does not make us sinners. We were sinners by nature, therefore we sinned.

Let me explain it this way. Remember, the word sin means to miss the mark or miss the road. A man that is lost continually misses the correct road because he is lost. He does not know which road to take in order to get to where he is going. But if I know where I am going and I miss the road, I am not lost. I just missed the road. All I have to do is turn around (repent) and get on the right road. When we sin as a believer we are not lost, we just missed our road. All we have to do is turn around and get back on the correct road.

For way too long, Christians have been brought under the bondage of sin by leaders who have continually kept them sin-conscious. Most Christians are told that the Holy Spirit is here to continually show us our sin. But that is not what the Bible says. Revelation 12:10 says that Satan is the accuser of the brethren. Satan is the one that continually makes you conscious of your sin. He is your accuser. Christ is your defender. As Jesus was giving His last instructions to his disciples, He told them that He was going to send the Holy Spirit to them. Jesus said that the Holy Spirit would convict of three things. "And when He has come, He will convict the world of sin and of righteousness and of judgment" (John 16:8-9).

I know that I just told you that it was Satan who convicts us of sin and you are thinking that I made a mistake. But Jesus goes on to explain what He means. In the next verse He says, "Of sin, because they do not believe in Me." So, what is the sin that the Holy Spirit convicts us of? He convicts us of not believing in Christ. That is how you came to Christ. The Holy Spirit convicted you. According to John 3, man is condemned because he does not believe in Christ, not because of his sinful acts. The Holy Spirit convicts us and draws us to Christ for salvation. But that is not all the Holy Spirit convicts us of. He convicts us of our righteousness. He is our defender. In John 16:10, Jesus goes on to say that the Holy Spirit convicts "of righteousness, because I go to My Father, and you see Me no more." When Jesus rose from the dead, He took His blood into the heavenly Holy of Holies and sprinkled the mercy seat with His own blood. This separated us from our sins forever. If you take away our sin -- all that is wrong is gone and all that remains is right. The Holy Spirit convicts us that we are righteous because Christ took our sin and paid our debt. We need to become convicted of our righteousness. Jesus has made us righteous. Sin has no place in the believer's life.

Romans 6 tells us that we have died to sin and that our sinful life was buried with Christ. Notice that this is in the past tense. It is not that our sinful life will be buried with Christ sometime in the future; it was buried. It has already taken place. "What shall we say then? Shall we continue in sin that grace may abound? Certainly not! How shall we who died to sin live any longer in it? Or do you not know that as many of us as were baptized into Christ Jesus were baptized into His death? Therefore, we were buried with Him through baptism into death, that just as Christ was raised from the dead by the glory of the Father, even so we also should walk in newness of life. For if we have been united together in the likeness of His death, certainly we also shall be in the likeness of His resurrection, knowing this, that our old man was crucified with Him, that the body of sin might be done away with, that we should no longer be slaves of sin. For he who has died has been freed from sin" (Romans 6:1-7).

We are free from sin. It has no place in us. Dead men cannot sin. You have never seen a corpse stealing or committing adultery. It is impossible because they are dead. That is why a Christian cannot sin. We are dead and dead men cannot sin. I may not know what you have done this week, but I know where the real you lives. If you are a born-again believer in the Lord Jesus Christ, you are seated with Him in heavenly places and you cannot sin. That is exactly what Ephesians 2:4-6 says. "By His grace, He has seated you in Christ Jesus at the right hand of the Father." Your spirit is seated in Christ right now. This is not truth for the future. You are seated in Christ right now, today.

That is what the apostle John is speaking of in 1 John 3:9, when he says, "Whoever has been born of God does not sin, for His seed remains in him; and he cannot sin, because he has been born of God." The real you is the spirit you. That is the part that is eternal. Your spirit man is eternal. Your spirit man is seated with Christ and cannot sin. Your spirit is totally righteous and cannot sin.

When Jesus saved you, He sealed you and the real you cannot sin. We express this truth at funerals when we talk to our children. We tell them, "That is not Uncle Bob; that is just his body. Uncle Bob has gone home to be with Jesus. That is just his empty house." We must explain to them that what is lying before them is not the "real" person. We know these fleshly bodies are not us.

We are moving out of these houses someday. I do not care about having a fancy casket when I die. I will not be in that box!

If you were to go with me to where I grew up on the south side of Dallas, you would see the little house in which I was raised. It is just a small, wood frame house! The last time we drove by that house, the Johnson grass was higher than the windows. I did not say, "Oh, my house. I need to fix that up." Instead, I said, "Praise God I don't live here anymore." Our fleshly body is not who we are. It is just where we live right now. Our flesh will one day die. The flesh tells us to sin, but our spirit reminds us that we are the righteousness of God in Christ -- we are sinless.

When we were created in the image of God, we were created a triune entity like God. God consists of Father, Son, and Holy Spirit. We are a spirit, we have a soul (mind, will and emotions) and live in body. When we came to Jesus, our spirit was reborn (born-again) and we were made perfect. All our sin was forgiven, and we were seated in heavenly places with Christ Jesus. If you are in Christ, you are wherever He is - seated next to the Father. Sin cannot be found in that place. When our spirit man rules, sin becomes obsolete. When you have the best, the artificial cannot entice you. Because of who we are, we cannot "miss the mark" in our real essence of being -- our spirit. However, we do find that we sin in this body in which we dwell. Paul the apostle says, "Now if I do what I will not to do, it is no longer I who do it, but sin that dwells in me" (Romans 7:20). He continues the thought in the next verses, "For I delight in the law of God according to the inward man. But I see another law in my members, warring against the law of my mind and bringing me into captivity to the law of sin which is in my members. O wretched man that I am! Who will deliver me from this body of death? I thank God-- through Jesus Christ our Lord! So then, with the mind I myself serve the law of God, but with the flesh the law of sin." Although we find a chapter break in the text, that break was not there in the original letter. Romans 8:1 continues this thought: "There is therefore now no condemnation to those who are in Christ Jesus, who do not walk according to the flesh, but according to the Spirit." There is no condemnation because Jesus was condemned in our place. He became our sin, and we became His righteousness. Our spirit is totally righteous and dwells in Christ.

Our responsibility as believers is to work out this spirit righteousness into our soul and body. We must bring the reality of who we are in Christ (righteous) into our physical life. Philippians 2:12 says, 'Therefore, my beloved, as you have always obeyed, not as in my presence only, but now much more in my absence, work out your own salvation with fear and trembling." For years, many churches have taught that you must work out your own salvation by works. That is not what Paul is addressing. He says that you are righteous and your spirit man is perfect. You must work that out in your mind, your will and your emotions. You must work out your salvation. Move it from theory and into reality. It is not enough for you to say, "I am the righteousness of God." He wants you to work that out in your everyday living. Work that out in your workplace, your family . . . in this real world. Too many Christians use their righteousness as an escape and rationalization for sin in this world. He did not make us righteous so we could sin. He says, "You are righteous. Now, act like it!" We must determine to not miss the mark -- not to miss the road of righteousness. We must declare a conscious war against sin and renew our mind on the Word of God.

# CHAPTER 3

# REPENTANCE

*Do you despise the riches of His goodness, forbearance, and longsuffering, not knowing that the goodness of God leads you to repentance?*
Romans 2:4

Repentance is one of those words that that the Church world casually tosses around as if everyone knows the meaning. Because of this casual treatment the true meaning of the word is often overshadowed by the continued use of the word in the church vernacular. As is true of most teaching, the pendulum swings to great extremes in defining this term repentance. To some, it is as casual a thing as changing your mind about a menu choice at lunch. While to others, it is of such deep feeling that it requires great agony of soul. So, it seems only fitting that we reason together and see if we can discover the true meaning of repentance.

## WHAT REPENTANCE IS NOT!

As we begin this study, let us first examine what repentance is not. It is not simple sorrow or penitence. Although this is possibly the most often used idea of repentance, it is also most likely the least true definition. When most people use the word repentance this is what they are implying. To most people repentance is about shame and regret.

This is the kind of thing every parent sees in raising their children. When we catch our children in a wrong, they tell us that they are sorry. What they most often really mean is that they are sorry that they got caught. They may even be sorry that they have disappointed us. But this sorrow is not Scriptural repentance. In 2 Corinthians 7:9-10, Paul explains that true godly sorrow always leads to true godly repentance. Sorrow and repentance are not synonymous. You can be sorry without that sorrow leading to repentance.

Penitence is a thing the church has added to the Gospel. Penitent is defined as being sorry or ashamed for having done wrong and being willing to atone. Penitence says, "I am so sorry that I have done this wrong that I want to do something to make it right." While this is a good thing to do in our relationship with other people, it is the wrong attitude in our relationship with God. A penitent spirit fails to acknowledge that there is nothing left to do to atone for my sins. Christ has done it all. Even though it might make me feel better to do something, there is nothing I can do. My sins are forgiven because of what Christ did on the cross of Calvary. Penitence puts a requirement on forgiveness. Penitence requires that I make some kind of payment or sacrifice to gain my forgiveness. Penitence has nothing to do with true repentance. Repentance is a God-ordained thing; penitence is something that man has created. We think that if we go and do these things, it will somehow cause God to forgive us. That is works, not grace. That is religion, not relationship.

Religion is any activity that we perform in an attempt to make ourselves acceptable to God. Repentance is not a condition of the soul, or change of heart, that makes the sinner acceptable to God. Most of us grew up with the mindset that if there was sin in our life, then we were unacceptable to God. We were told that when we sinned God turned His back to us or would not hear us. That is not true for us as New Covenant believers in Christ. As we learned in our lesson on sin, Isaiah says that our sin separates us, so that God cannot hear. But that is before the cross. That is before the New Covenant was established. Romans 8 tells us that there is absolutely nothing that can separate us from the love of God.

Not only can nothing separate us, nothing we do can make us unacceptable to God. Conversely, there is nothing we can do to make ourselves acceptable to God. Typically, when the church has moved into a focus on holiness, she has at the same time moved into law. The law says that if you do certain things, God accepts you. If you do not do these things, then God will not accept you. Much of the church world today believes that if you are not baptized as an infant, you are not part of the Kingdom. Sometime later you go to classes and learn basic teachings and validate what was done to you as an infant. But again, that is religion; it is not repentance. Being baptized as an infant does not make you a Christian. It just makes you cry. According to the Scripture, a baby is sanctified not by that water, but by the faith of believing parents. There comes a point in our development where we become conscious of our sin. At that point we become accountable for our own deeds. When we become conscious of our sin, repentance is needed. We acknowledge that we are on the wrong path. We have missed the mark. But that repentance does not give us merit with God. It has no merit of its own. It is simply a recognition of our sin and our need for a Savior. That recognition leads us to put our faith in Christ as our savior.

Many people feel that the greater the show of the repentance, the greater impact it has. In the Old Testament, we find the phrase "sackcloth and ashes." If a person wanted to show the depth of his repentance, he would put on coarse clothing and throw ashes from the fire on his head. He would repeatedly say, "I am nothing." This is an Old Covenant expression of sorrow and repentance to God. It was an act of humility. However, it has no place in the New Covenant. If you were to say that you are nothing today --after all the Lord Jesus Christ has done for you -- then you would be insulting Him and His grace. He doesn't say that you are nothing. He says that you are a saint. If you are a follower of Christ, you are a saint. You should agree with Him.

New Testament repentance is not wailing and crying out to God for mercy. My wife and I were in a meeting some years ago where the evangelist was really moving the crowd into an emotional state. He would say, "If you are really repenting, why am I not hearing you? Why are you not crying out to God?" God is not impressed by your screaming. Repentance is not validated by your tears. It is not valid because you made yourself feel bad about it. Mercy has already been extended to you. It was His mercy that dealt with your sin. His mercy has already been extended to its fullest capacity. You don't have to beg for it or cry out for it. All you have to do is receive it. In reality, if you must do anything to earn forgiveness, it is not really mercy.

Although repentance may involve the emotions and will always involve the heart, it is not simply an emotion. Emotion may be a symptom of repentance, but repentance is not an emotion. A man who mentored me for years once said, "If someone comes to Christ without tears, then it is not valid." To validate his position, he used the parable of the sower and the seed. In that story, the second group of seeds fell on stony ground. The plant immediately sprang up. But when the sun came out, it dried up and died. Jesus said that these represent those who receive the gospel with joy, but when difficulty arises, they fall away. It says that they received the word with joy. My friend said, "If you receive the Word with joy, it is not valid. You have to come crying." As much as I respect this dear saint of God, that statement is not true. Many different emotions may accompany true repentance. There may be sorrow, but true repentance many times also includes a deep sense of joy. We had missed the road -- lost our way -- and now we see the road. Turning back to the right path should produce joy. But no matter what emotion we experience, repentance is not an emotion. It is a decision.

Repentance is not simply regret or remorse either, because repentance is not a looking backwards. True repentance is always looking forward. It is not about what we have done in the past. Truthfully, it is about what we are going to do in the future. It is not some contrition wherein we obtain forgiveness and favor. In Psalm 51, David says that God does not require sacrifice, but a broken and contrite heart. Contrition means that I am really, really worked up about this and my heart is broken. I am so worked up that I decide to change my mindset and behavior in this matter. It is a change of desire. Oftentimes, we can be truly sorry about something only to turn around and do the same thing a few minutes later. That is because we are looking at the past. We are looking backwards. But true repentance looks forward.

## SO WHAT IS REPENTANCE?

However, we choose to define repentance, that definition must be compatible with New Testament principles of grace. Repentance must attach itself to grace. Anything that is not compatible with grace is not New Testament repentance. Grace says that God has done all the work. Anything that says that I must do some of the work to get forgiveness is not in accordance with New Testament scripture.

But while refusing to exalt repentance at the cost of grace, we must guard against the other extreme of reducing repentance to a mere mental change or intellectual function. Repentance is not just a change of mind. It involves a change of mind, but it is much deeper than that. I have heard it flippantly taught that every time you change your mind about something, you are repenting. Although repentance means to change the mind, it is deeper than a casual change of mind. It is not this exalted thing wherein we somehow earn forgiveness. But neither is it a casual change of mind like changing your mind about what shirt you are going to wear.

Repentance is not simply changing our mind in an intellectual sense. God must have reality. He is not looking for religion. God functions and operates in reality. If He demands "a change of mind," it is not of the intellectual faculty that He speaks. Some teach that you can repent like you change channels on the television. The real meaning of this word speaks of changing the man himself, the real man. Repentance involves a change of mindset in the real person. It is this real person change that Paul speaks of in Romans when he says, "I myself, with the mind, serve the law of God" (Romans 7:25). He is talking about serving God with his essence – that which is really "me." Repentance is the turning of the mind or heart – the man himself. It is this inner person that changes in true repentance.

## THREE GREEK WORDS

There are three Greek words used in the original New Testament text to denote repentance. The most shallow of these is the verb *metamelomai*. According to *Vine's Expository Dictionary*, this word literally means: a change of mind, such as to produce regret or even remorse on account of sin, but not necessarily a change of heart. This is the word used to explain how Judas felt after betraying Christ. Matthew 27:3 says that he repented or that he was remorseful. He recognized that he had sinned and was sorry for what he had done. This word is only used six times in the entire New Testament. It speaks of regret or sorrow for sin.

The second word we will examine is the Greek word *metanoeo*, which literally means to "think afterwards." This word means to rethink a thing and, in this rethinking, have a change of mind. It means: to have a change of heart after rethinking an action. This word is used thirty-four times in the New Testament and it always implies a change for the better. A perfect example of the use of this word is found in Revelation 2:5. The Lord is addressing the Church of Ephesus and He first tells her to think about how things once were. "Remember, therefore from where you have fallen." He is telling them to think about how their love has changed. Then He says, "repent and do the first works." Notice the progression: think about what you have done, change your thinking in this matter, and then change your behavior. That is what this word means. Think about what you have done and what you are doing. Think about what you once had and then change your mind about what you are going to do.

The final word is the Greek word *metanoia*. This word is the noun form of the preceding word and is used in the New Testament an additional twenty-four times. It is used of true repentance; a change of mind and purpose and life.

## A CHANGE OF PURPOSE

So, we see that repentance is a change of purpose, arising from a change of circumstances or from dissatisfaction with a former purpose and prompting a change of action. John the Baptist came preaching repentance. He proclaimed, "Repent for the kingdom of heaven is at hand!" He is telling the children of Israel to think about how they are living. They are living as though the coming kingdom was a long way off. They are not living according to the plans, purposes, and laws of God. They have to repent - to change their mind. Change their purpose because their purpose is not way off in the future – it is NOW! He is saying that they need to change their way of thinking.

Prophets of old told Israel to repent. If you read the prophecies, they all speak of a change of a particular action. They call forth repentance saying, "You have done . . . " A simple, visible illustration of this message is found in the prophet Nathan speaking to King David. Nathan calls for David's repentance. Nathan does not walk into the throne room and tell David to repent. Instead, he tells a story. He says that there was a wealthy man who had a lot of sheep. His neighbor was a poor farmer who had only one little lamb. One night, some friends of the rich man came for a visit. He decided to have lamb chops. As opposed to killing one of his hundreds of sheep, he went to his neighbor's farm and killed the neighbor's only lamb. David rose from his throne and demanded that justice be done to the man. Nathan told David that he was the man. He was telling David to think about what he had done and change his mindset about what he had done.

2 Chronicle 7:14 is a verse we often use in calling the Church to repentance, even though it has nothing to do with the Church and is an Old Covenant verse. It reads, "If My people who are called by My name will humble themselves and pray and seek My face and turn from their wicked ways, then I will hear from heaven and will forgive their sin and heal their land." This verse calls for a specific repentance. When we recognize that we have done wrong, it is humbling. Pride oftentimes keeps men from repenting. This is a call to repentance; remember, repent, and

change behavior. However, we need to keep in mind that this is an old covenant passage. It implies that God does not hear our prayers and was true of the old covenant. But we have a new and better covenant that promises that He will never leave us nor forsake us. Because of the blood of Jesus, nothing can separate us from God.

In Matthew 5-7, we find Jesus' longest teaching. We call this teaching the Sermon on the Mount. In that sermon, Jesus is exposing the inability of the Law to produce righteousness. He is showing the Jewish people that the law addresses action rather than heart or mindset. He continually says, "You have heard it said ... but I say ... ". Jesus said, "You have heard it said that thou shalt not commit adultery, but I say to you, if the heart is adulterous, you have committed adultery already" (Matthew 5:28). He is telling them that the act of adultery happens because of an adulterous heart. If you change the heart, change the mindset, you will produce a change of action. The promise of the Father in the Old Testament was that He was going to put a new heart in His people. "I will give you a new heart and put a new spirit within you; I will take the heart of stone out of your flesh and give you a heart of flesh. I will put My Spirit within you and cause you to walk in My statutes and you will keep My judgments and do them" (Ezekiel 36:26-27).

What a perfect picture of the new covenant we have in Christ Jesus. He changes us on the inside and this change on the inside causes a change in behavior. We have a tendency to misinterpret the Sermon on the Mount and simply add new law to old law. You can never address the heart with the law. The heart will not be molded by the law. It will only be molded by relationship. Our heart is molded by relationship with Christ.

Under the old covenant, we have what we will call **repentance from**. God was continually telling Israel to repent from their wicked ways and the things that they were doing wrong. As you read the prophets, they continually told the people to repent (turn from) their sin and unrighteousness. Even though John the Baptist is found in the New Testament, he is an Old Testament prophet. He is the last Old Testament prophet, and he prepared the way for the New Covenant. But he is still preaching Old Testament repentance -- the Promise of the Father had not yet come. He is telling the people to repent from their sin because Messiah is corning.

On the other hand, the characteristic of gospel (good news) repentance is **repentance to**. The New Testament repentance principle is not just looking back at the past and recognizing our sin. It is a change of mindset that causes a change in the course in which we are going. We should not be focused on what we have done wrong; those wrongs are covered by the blood of Christ and God does not even remember them. We tend to focus on those things of which Jesus has washed us and the Father does not even remember those things. Just before Jesus went to the cross, He was telling His disciples about what to expect. He told them that He was going away, but that He was going to send them another Helper - the Holy Spirit. He says that when the Holy Spirit comes, He will convict of three things: sin, righteousness and judgment (John 16:8-11). He says that the Holy Spirit will convict us of our sin and the sin is that we do not believe in the Lord Jesus Christ. It does not say that He will convict us of our sins, but of our sin - that we do not believe in Jesus. Today, the Holy Spirit is trying to convict us that we are not truly and affectively believing in the Lord Jesus Christ. We do not believe that He took our sin in His body on the tree, paid the debt for it and there no longer remains a sacrificial offering for sin. We have difficulty believing that He effectively dealt with our sin.

We think that we somehow must add to that which He accomplished. We must do some penance in order to be forgiven. The Holy Spirit continually has to convict us of our unbelief. When He convicts us of our unbelief, it is to cause us to begin to believe. In John 16:10, Jesus says that the Holy Spirit also comes to convict us of righteousness. Notice that it does not say that He will convict us of unrighteousness, but righteousness. He says that the Holy Spirit will convict of righteousness, because Christ is going to the Father. He is foretelling what Paul addresses later. Jesus was raised from the dead and seated at the right hand of the Father. We are in Christ, and He has raised us up and seated us in heavenly places with Christ Jesus. The Holy Spirit has to convict us of this fact. When we are convicted of this truth, there is a repentance that occurs inside of us that has nothing to do with wailing and weeping. A repentance occurs that changes our thought process. We no longer think the same way. We do not think as mere humans for we have become "partakers of the divine nature" (2 Peter 1:4). We don't just act different – we **ARE** different.

There was once a man traveling to a friend's house at night. He was making his way across a large grassland. Using the friend's farmhouse as a landmark, he heads toward the light of the farmhouse. He soon crosses paths with another traveler. The fellow traveler asks him where he is going. He says that he is heading to his friend's farmhouse and points to a light shining in the distance. The traveler tells him, "That is not your friend's farmhouse. That is a campsite of a friend of mine." The traveler realizes that to continue his course would be a mistake. This realization is repentance from. The man halts his travel and contemplates what to do. Before long another traveler comes along and shows him the actual light of his friend's farmhouse sitting off in the distance. The traveler sets out in the new direction; headed toward the light of the farmhouse. This is repentance to or towards. It would have been of no benefit to the traveler to sit on a rock and cry when he realized that he had gone the wrong way. It would not change anything. If he had said, "I am so sorry that I took the wrong course," it would not have changed anything either. If he was going to his friend's farmhouse for supper, his friend is not going to want to hear how sorry he is and how bad he felt for going the wrong way. The friend just wants him to get on the correct path and get to his house for supper.

That is a picture of true repentance. In the course of our life, we often go after the wrong lights. When God brings knowledge into our life that shows us that we are on the wrong path, He is not calling for sackcloth and ashes. He is not calling for us to be sorry. He is calling for us to change the way we think, so we can change the direction of our life. When the man found that he was going the wrong direction, there was a repentance from. He believed the counsel that he was going in the wrong direction. He did not know where he was going next, but he knew he was not going to continue on his previous course. When he received further knowledge of where his friend's house was located, there was repentance towards. Biblical repentance involved repentance from and repentance towards.

## GODLY REPENTANCE IS NECESSARY FOR SALVATION

Man cannot be saved without repentance because there must be a changing of his thinking. There must be a changing of the guard in the way he thinks. A perfect example of this can be found with the rich, young ruler. The rich, young ruler came to Jesus and Jesus called for repentance even though He never used the word, "repentance". The young man asked Jesus, "What must I do to inherit the Kingdom?" Jesus told him to keep the whole law. The young man said, "I have kept it since my youth." Then Jesus calls for repentance. He calls for a change in thinking. He tells the young ruler, "Go sell all that you have, give it to the poor and follow Me." He does not tell him, "Repent!" But what He demands requires repentance. The young man will have to change the way he is thinking. He is thinking that his resources are his source. But Jesus is saying, "I am going to be your source. You must change your thinking. You must become dependent upon Me. You must change your thinking about My kingdom, for My kingdom is not a "getting" kingdom. My kingdom is a "giving" kingdom. In order to enter the kingdom, there had to be a change in the young man's thinking. There had to be repentance.

In the third chapter of Acts, Peter and John heal a lame man. When the people are astonished, Peter begins to preach Christ to them. He invites them to partake of the New Covenant. In verse 19, we find these words, "Repent therefore and be converted, that your sins may be blotted out, so that times of refreshing may come from the presence of the Lord." This does not say that this is done over and over. Your sins are blotted out once. The Scripture says that when Jesus blots out your sin, He blots them all out. He forgives them and removes them as far as the east is from the west. He removes them so effectively that He remembers them no more (Psalm 103:12). This is a hard truth for most Christians to grasp, for it requires that we humble ourselves and recognize that this is all grace. There is nothing I do. Once I come to Christ, my sins are no longer remembered.

## REPENTANCE AND GRACE

This is hard for most Christians because they have been taught that confession is required for forgiveness. They have been drilled on I John 1:9. "If we confess our sins, He is faithful and just to forgive us our sins and to cleanse us from all unrighteousness." They have been taught that every day they must give an account of their sins and confess them to God. Some have even been taught to write these sins down and keep an accurate account. However, this is the only place in the New Testament where confession is required for forgiveness of sin. One of the rules of theology is that you never build doctrine upon one verse. Yet, there is no other verse in the entire New Testament that tells you that you must confess your sins in order to be forgiven of your sins. So, the question becomes, what does this verse really mean?

I grew up in the Baptist church. One thing the Baptists understand very clearly is the doctrine of the security of the believer. We clearly understood salvation by grace. We understood that we were not forgiven by our own works, but by what Ephesians. 2:8-9 says, "For by grace you have been saved through faith and that not of yourselves; it is the gift of God, not of works, lest anyone should boast." I firmly believe that there is no other doctrine as foundational to living the Christian life as this one.

Early on in my first pastorate, I had a deacon come and explain to me his position on confession. He told me that if people confessed their sins, they were forgiven. But if they did not confess their sins, they were not forgiven. In actuality, he was the only person I ever spoke with about confession that was honest about his interpretation of 1 John 1:9. You see, if you interpret this verse like most folks do, you have to be willing to accept the consequences of NOT confessing. You must be willing to say, "If I do not confess my sins, He is faithful and just and will NOT forgive me of my sins or cleanse me from all my unrighteousness." But the question arises, "How many unforgiven sins does it take to send me to hell?" Just one. I asked this brother, "What if in your life, you miss just one sin?" He told me that he would go to hell. Now, that really concerns me because my memory is not that good. Out of all the sins I have committed in my lifetime, I cannot have failed to confess even one. Can you imagine standing before God on judgment day and hearing Him say, "I would like to let you in, but on Thursday, January 10, 1997, at 3 p.m. you sinned and never confessed it. You are sentenced to hell." That simply does not align with the New Testament.

If anyone tells you that a verse has a particular meaning, take the ramifications out to the *n*th degree and see if it holds water. If it does not sound right and does not match up with the rest of Scripture, it is not right. You have been misinformed. Always translate Scripture with other Scripture.

What He is talking about in I John 1:9 is the same thing we are talking about here. Repent and be converted. Once you are converted, repentance changes. As a believer, I am not repenting to be converted, or that my sins can be blotted out, or that I can have times of refreshing with the Lord. If I think that way, God's presence, and God's refreshing spirit upon me are dependent upon my performance. If someone else acts better than I do, then they get more love from the Father than I do. That may be the way the world operates, but it is not the way God operates. If my performance is the determining factor, it is no longer grace. Anything you must earn is not grace, no matter how you earn it. Faith itself can be a work if you think you must produce it. Even in your salvation, faith is not your work. Ephesians 2:8 says, "For by grace you have been saved through faith and that not of yourselves; it is the gift of God." He required faith from you for salvation. But God knew that you did not have faith. So, He gave you the faith that you needed, so that you could access the grace. God tells us that He sets before us life and death. It is a quiz, but He gives us the answer – choose life and here is the faith with which to choose!

In Acts 2, we find Peter preaching to the crowd in Jerusalem. They ask, "What must we do to be saved?" Peter responds, "Repent and let every one of you be baptized in the name of Jesus Christ for the remission of sins." Without repentance, there is no salvation. Your sins are blotted out with repentance. When you come and tell God how sorry you are, it is not repentance. Many people tell God how sorry they are, but their lives never change. Repentance is the change of heart and mind that says, "I don't want to do that anymore. I see the error of my own way. I want to walk in God's way." It is not simply saying, "I am not going to do that anymore." We say that easily. It is the change of heart that says, "I don't even WANT to do that anymore. It holds no attraction to me." Once you change your desire, it is no longer a draw on you. Sin operates through your desires. When you change the desire (the purpose and intents of the heart), sin no longer appeals to you. That is why the Bible says that when Satan came to Jesus, he found nothing in Him. There were no wrong desires that could be ignited into sin.

Some of the most adamant anti-smokers are ex-smokers. They cannot stand for anyone to smoke in their presence. It is not that they have trouble saying, "No!" They do not want cigarettes anymore. Once the desire leaves, then it is no longer a temptation. Now, the thing that once captivated them angers them. They have had a change of mindset that resulted in a change of behavior.

This change of mind in repentance is often accompanied by a certain sense of sorrow for having done the wrongs. But we must be careful because there is godly sorrow and worldly sorrow. If our sorrow does not lead to a true repentance, it is simply worldly or soulful sorrow. But godly sorrow is a good thing for it leads us to repentance. In Paul's second letter to his friends at Corinth, he says, "Now I rejoice, not that you were made sorry, but that your sorrow led to repentance. For you were made sorry in a godly manner, that you might suffer loss from us in nothing. For godly sorrow produces repentance leading to salvation, not

3 Repentance

to be regretted; but the sorrow of the world produces death" (2 Corinthian 7:9-10). Ungodly sorrow just makes you feel bad. God does not want to make you feel bad. He wants you to move forward in your journey with Him. In the process of revelation, you may feel bad for all the wasted years. Most new revelation from the Lord involves a godly sorrow. We say, "I can't believe I've walked all these years and didn't do that." But that sorrow is not repentance. It just leads us to repentance.

Many years ago, my son, Sam, was playing football for his high school. On the way to one of his games, the Lord told me to pray for protection over him against injury. If you know anything about athletes, you know that they have a period before the game where they get their "game face" on. They focus on what they are going to do and how they will do it. Sam was in this mode on the way to the game. So, as opposed to doing what I knew I needed to do and interrupting his schedule, I let him proceed in getting ready for the game. In the second quarter, he sprained his wrist. There was a sorrow in my heart because I knew that it did not have to happen. As a father, I should not have allowed that to happen, but I did. God told me to pray because He knew what was coming. How much good would it have done for me to sit in the bleachers and cry when I saw them take him off the field and put that ice on his wrist? That would not have changed a single thing. There had to be a change in my heart that said, "That is not going to happen again." The Lord does not want us wailing and moaning about what did not happen. He wants us to say, "Next time, Lord, we will take care of these things."

Man was created for LIFE ... not just life, but the fullness of life. Because of the Fall of Adam and Eve, man has not been living in LIFE. Man has been living in sin and death. Romans 3:23 says, "For all have sinned and fall short of the glory of God." That word ALL is a big word. It includes every person who has ever lived, except Christ. And Romans 6:23 says, "For the wages of sin is death, but the gift of God is eternal life in Christ Jesus our Lord." The penalty of sin is the loss of the fullness of life. But Christ bore that penalty for us. He became sin for us and set us free to live life to the fullest. Romans 8:2 says, "For the law of the Spirit of life in Christ Jesus has made me free from the law of sin and death." True repentance is a change of the inner man. The inner essence - heart, mind and soul - must change. There must be a change of the very purpose of life.

We must **repent from** this world's corrupt thinking and purposes

We must **repent to** God's life-giving thinking and purposes.

## HOW DOES REPENTANCE OCCUR?

This kind of repentance is laid out for us by the apostle Paul in Romans 12:1-2. "I beseech you therefore, brethren, by the mercies of God, that you present your bodies a living sacrifice, holy, acceptable to God, which is your reasonable service." He is calling for repentance from our old selfish lifestyle when he speaks of a living sacrifice. Jesus told us that if we want to follow Him, we must deny ourselves, take up our cross and follow Him. The cross is an instrument of death; no matter how beautiful we make it look in our jewelry. We are to die to our own selfish ways and plans.

When he says, *holy, acceptable to God*, he is calling for a **repentance to** a Godly lifestyle that is a reasonable thing. This word holy means "wholly other or totally different." We are to live a life that is totally different from what other people live. Our mindset and lifestyle is not of this world. This new life is acceptable because it is a **repentance to** God. It is saying, "I am sacrificing my ways, my thinking and the world's principles. I am living according to Your system. There has been a change of mind in me."

But he does not stop there, he reiterates this point. "And do not be conformed to this world, but be transformed by the renewing of your mind, that you may prove what is that good and acceptable and perfect will of God." When He says do not be conformed to this world, He uses the word Greek word *cosmos* and it speaks of this world's system. Here he is addressing **repentance from**. Paul is saying that we must turn from this world's system in all our thinking. We must not think like this world's system thinks. But he not only shows us what light not to follow, he points to the true light by which we can direct our steps and find our way. Repentance acknowledges wrong thinking and change to correct thinking.

## TRANSFORMED THINKING

When He tells us to be transformed by the renewing of your mind, he is addressing **repentance to**. This renewing of your mind and repentance are synonymous. As I get God's thoughts into me, there will be repentance from my thoughts and repentance to His thoughts. Repentance is a continual thing. Many times, we get people worked up during ministry time so that they will make a show of their repentance. But in reality, true repentance is not like that. True repentance is a daily, habitual thing. In the process of being conformed to the image of Christ, I am repenting **from things** and **to things** all the time. It is not an emotional thing. It is a knowledge thing; an understanding thing; a revelation thing. We are on a journey of revelation; learning who we are in Christ.

We must repent of thinking that we are sinners. Most of us think we must repent as sinners. But the Scriptures tell us that as believers in Christ we are not sinners; we are saints. Paul continually refers to the church as those who are called saints. If you are still calling yourself a sinner, you must repent. You are not agreeing with God. If you are not agreeing with God on any issue, you must repent of that thinking. God says that you were a sinner, but His Holy Spirit came into you, His Son paid the price for you, and you are the temple of the Holy Spirit and He calls you a saint! You must stop thinking of yourself as a sinner and begin thinking of yourself as a righteous child of God.

Saints of God have no sin in them because Christ took their sin. I John 1:8 says that he who says that he has no sin is a liar and the truth is not in him. But this verse is not talking about us as Christians being sinners. This verse is addressing the fact that sinners need a savior. If we do not believe that we have sin and therefore don't need a Savior, then we are liars. We do have sin and we do need a Savior. That is why we came to Christ; we had a sin issue. If a person believes that he is not a sinner, he will never come to Christ for salvation. But if he understands that he is a sinner and confesses his sin, God is faithful and just to forgive those sins and cleanse him from all unrighteousness. God is faithful and just. That justice demanded death for sin. Christ became sin and died for us. Because God is just, He cannot hold us accountable for that which Christ has already been convicted. Christ has already paid our debt - there is no debt left to pay. This fact should create a great well of joy and thanksgiving to rise up within our heart.

## AREAS OF REPENTANCE FOR BELIEVERS

In the first few chapters of the book of Revelation, we find Christ's letters to the seven churches. All but two of these letters call for repentance. Only Smyrna and Philadelphia escape the call. The important thing for us to remember is that these calls for repentance are addressed to believers. These are not calls to repentance for salvation. These are calls to Christians to repent -- to change their mindset and heart.

In His first letter, Christ writes to the church at Ephesus. He encourages them for their good work, but He says He has a problem with their heart. "Nevertheless, I have this against you, that you have left your first love. Remember therefore from where you have fallen; repent and do the first works, or else I will come to you quickly and remove your lampstand from its place--unless you repent" (Revelation 2:4-5). He tells us to remember the love we once had. He does not tell us to remember how bad we have been. Remember how it once was.

Remember the love relationship we had with Him in the beginning. Then, He tells us to repent - change our thinking - quit living for ourselves and our interests. True love lives for the other person. He is calling us back to a love relationship with Him. He is reiterating what 1 Corinthians 13 says, "And now abide faith, hope, love, these three; but the greatest of these is love." The most important thing in the kingdom is love. When we change our mind and heart, we will begin to do the works that accompany that change of heart. We will begin to do the first works.

## 3 Repentance

In His letter to the church at Pergamos, He addresses the issue of compromise in the Church and an unwillingness to stand for what is right. He is telling them that they have developed wrong thinking and they must repent – change their mind. "But I have a few things against you, because you have there those who hold the doctrine of Balaam, who taught Balak to put a stumbling block before the children of Israel, to eat things sacrificed to idols and to commit sexual immorality. Thus, you also have those who hold the doctrine of the Nicolaitans, which thing I hate. Repent, or else I will come to you quickly and will fight against them with the sword of My mouth" (Revelation 2:14-16).

Instead of dying to self and this world system, the Nicolaitans taught them to accept the world. The Nicolaitans followed in the ways of Balaam, the prophet, who caused Israel to stumble in faith. He had counseled Balak to use the wiles of sexual desire to divert Israel into sin. The Nicolaitans were a sect of the Gnostics. They taught all sorts of impure doctrines based upon their teaching that the physical world is not real. Therefore, what happens in the world doesn't really matter. They mixed pagan rites with Christian worship and taught that fornication and adultery were permissible, since this world is not real. The Gnostics always caused division in that they believed they had a higher knowledge. Allowing this spirit of pride and division to exist is just as dangerous as immorality. Christ calls for their repentance because they have allowed that spirit to stay. When we begin to think that we are "all important" and allow divisiveness to exist, we need to repent – change our heart and mindset. We must repent from our compromise and repent to His truth.

Next, Christ calls for repentance in the area of lewdness and immorality. To the church of Thyatira, He writes: "Nevertheless I have a few things against you, because you allow that woman Jezebel, who calls herself a prophetess, to teach and seduce My servants to commit sexual immorality and eat things sacrificed to idols. And I gave her time to repent of her sexual immorality and she did not repent" (Revelation 2:20-21). Gnosticism had gained great ground throughout the Roman Empire because it was compatible with Greek philosophy and Roman sensuality.

Over the years we have defined the Jezebel spirit as pertaining only to women. But the real issue is not women who are controlling. What He is concerned about here is lewdness and immorality. The problem with the spirit of Jezebel is that we are not offended by immorality anymore. As a matter of fact, we play into its draw. We have become too comfortable with the way the world does things. We have allowed those things into our heart. We have become so comfortable with them that they have become acceptable to us. Christ tells them that they must repent -- change their mind -- about this teaching. It is causing people to stumble in their walk with Christ. We too need to repent of allowing worldly thinking cloaked in Scripture to be a stumbling block to our faith. We live in a sexually driven world. We must guard our hearts to not fall into compromise. If we do fall, we need to be quick to repent. We need to repent of allowing this world's thinking and morals to enter our heart. Remember, we are not to conform to this world, but be transformed by the renewing of our mind. We need to repent from this world's ways of impurity and repent to God's ways of purity and life.

The Lord then turns his attention to dead works, hypocrisy, and self-righteousness. He warns the church at Sardis about these things. "These things says He who has the seven Spirits of God and the seven stars: I know your works, that you have a name that you are alive, but you are dead. Be watchful and strengthen the things which remain, that are ready to die, for I have not found your works perfect before God" (Revelation 3:1-2). Dead works are those works that we do, thinking that they will make us holy. We may look holy to those who see us, but our heart is wrong. These works only produce self-righteousness. We are only righteous because of what Christ did. When we understand our righteousness is by faith, we begin to realize our true righteousness. We act righteous because we are righteous in our inner being -- mindset and heart. We need to repent of our own self-righteousness and repent to Christ righteousness.

Finally, Christ warns us about being lukewarm. He says that He hates compromise. He would rather we were hot or cold. But we are lukewarm. Our faith and spiritual life are compromised and full of pretense. We have lost our fellowship with Christ. That is why He tells us in Revelation 3:20 that He will come in and have fellowship with us, if we will change our thinking. We have failed to acknowledge that He is always with us and never leaves us. We have taken that truth for granted and no longer listen to His voice. If we will turn from own ways and listen to His voice, we will once again be "hot" for God. If we want to get out of our lukewarm condition, we must get close to the fire. Our God is a consuming fire and He will melt away all compromise. We must repent from our hypocrisy and repent to living the fullness of life in Christ Jesus, who is our righteousness.

It is time for us to change our thinking. We must put off worldly thinking and put on the mind of Christ. If we are to conform to the image of Christ, we must repent.

*I beseech you therefore, brethren, by the mercies of God, that you present your bodies a living sacrifice, holy, acceptable to God, which is your reasonable service. And do not be conformed to this world, but be transformed by the renewing of your mind, that you may prove what is that good and acceptable and perfect will of God.*
Romans 12:1-2

# Chapter 4

# MERCY

*God's mercy and grace give me hope--
for myself, and for the world.*
Billy Graham

We began this series with a discussion of the vital principle we call life. Man was created by God in God's own image. He was God's self-portrait. But he was not just a creation. He was not just a work of art. He was created a living being in full possession of the God-life. In its very essence, this God-life includes the ability to make decisions. For man to possess the God-life, he had to be empowered with free will.

As an act of this free will, man chose knowledge over life. In the garden there were two trees: The Tree of Life and The Tree of Knowledge of good and evil. Man made the wrong choice and chose to ignore God's command. He did not believe that God's command was best for him. He fell into unbelief and chose to eat of the Tree of Knowledge. This sin of unbelief cost him the *vital principle*. Vital principle is the essence of life; it is the essence of God in us. With sin, we lost the vital principle. We lost life. All sin is unbelief at its core and unbelief always costs life.

Repentance is man's answer to his sin. As we discussed earlier, repentance is a change of heart, a change of purpose. Even though the Greek word literally means a change of mind, it carries a much deeper meaning. It means a change of mind in a more Eastern sense. It is a change in our very essence; it is a change in our way of seeing things; a change in our world view;

a change of paradigm; a change of the heart and purpose. This changing of the mind is a **change from** sin and a **change to** God. Repentance is man's response to sin, but that change must find footing in God's response.

God's response to sin involves a great paradox in the very essence of God. God is perfectly perfect. In Him there is nothing but infinite and absolute perfection, therefore there cannot be change. We change, but God cannot change. For infinite perfection to change, it would have to lose its perfection. That is why He tells the prophet Malachi, "For I am YAHWEH, I change not" (Malachi 3:6). And in his letter to the church, James says that in God "there is no variation or shadow of turning" (James 1:17). Even the prophet Balaam understood this principle. Although he was willing to allow his gifting to be purchased, he understood God's inability to change His essence. "God is not a man, that He should lie, nor a son of man, that He should repent" (Numbers 22:9). This inability to change creates a paradoxical issue in the very essence of God. He is perfectly just, while at the same time He is perfect love. His love and justice are in apposition to one another. His love demands that He forgive man and restore the vital principle. But His justice demands that man be separated from life.

## THE GREAT PARADOX

The most famous verse in the Bible is without doubt, John 3:16. In this verse, God tells us of His great love for us. "For God so loved the world that He gave His only begotten Son, that whoever believes in Him should not perish but have everlasting life." He desires to restore the vital principle of life back to man. He loves man so much that He was willing to sacrifice Himself to restore life back to man. He loves every man, woman, boy and girl on this planet with a perfect, sacrificial love. As a matter of fact, 2 Peter 3:9 specifically tells us that it is His desire to restore life back to every person on earth. "The Lord is not slow in keeping his promise, as some understand slowness. He is patient with you, not wanting anyone to perish, but everyone to come to repentance" (NIV).

We clearly see that God loves man so much that He does not want anyone to perish. He does not want anyone to miss the vital principle of life. God loves the world so much that He does not want to condemn anyone. That is an immense contrast to what many people believe. They think that God is some tyrant in the sky waiting to punish people. For too long, the church has acted as though God is trying to keep people out of heaven. But the opposite of that is true. God is love and because He loves, He is doing everything He can to get as many people as He can into heaven. God is not trying to keep people out; He is trying to get them in. God does not have some angelic attorney going over your life and looking for a reason to keep you out. That is not the heavenly reality. Many religious people are going to be quite shocked to discover some of those who get into heaven. They will most likely see many people that they are not expecting. These people may just barely get in; they may not receive vast rewards; they may be crownless for eternity. But God will be making every legitimate claim He can to get as many people as possible into heaven.

That is why Romans 10 says that all who call on the name of the Lord will be saved. People say, "You mean if somebody just called out to God to save them, they are saved?" If God can use it, He will use it. "Well, they never did anything. They never changed." That is not my responsibility, nor your responsibility. We have a tendency to say, "Well, they never changed, so hell gets them." God is saying, "They named me. I'm taking it . . . they are mine . . . they said they wanted Me to save them . . . so I did." Some will say, "But they didn't mean it." Who knows if they meant it or how deeply they meant it? Only God knows the answer to that.

Now let us look at it from another perspective. Suppose there is a multi-billionaire who is looking for a way to share his wealth. He says, "I will give a thousand dollars to anyone who asks me. My joy is to give away the thousand dollars." Now, let us suppose that someone does not really believe the billionaire will do what he says, but they ask for the thousand dollars anyway. They do not really expect anything to happen. Their request is almost in jest. But if it is the billionaire's joy to give away the thousand dollars, what is he going to do? Even though the person asking does not really believe it is going to happen, it does not matter. The billionaire does not care. It is his joy to give. He has said, "If you ask, I'll give it to you." Now, you need to keep that in mind. God has said that it is His desire that none should perish and that all should come to repentance. It is God's great desire that no one have to suffer the consequence of hell. His great love compels Him to welcome everyone possible into His family.

There is no doubt that our God is a loving God. But He is also infinitely and perfectly just. Isaiah 45:21 declares, "And there is no other God besides Me, a just God." And in the Book of Revelation, the apostle, John, sees a host of saints praising God. They sing, "Just and true are Your ways" (Revelation 15:3). In the same way that God is love, He is just and true. Jesus Himself said, "I am the Way, the Truth and the Life" (John 14:6). He is the Truth because He and the Father are One and the Father is just and true. God's justice is a pure justice in the same way that His love is pure love.

This is where the dilemma erupts. His justness will not allow His love to simply overlook sin. Numbers 14:18 says, "The LORD is longsuffering and abundant in mercy, forgiving iniquity and transgression." What a beautiful picture of God's infinite love. However, the verse does not end there. It continues, "But He by no means clears the guilty, visiting the iniquity of the fathers on the children to the third and fourth generation." The perfect love is offset by perfect justice. His justice demands payment and refuses to simply overlook the sin. God is saying, "If you are guilty, I am not going to simply forget it. I am not just going to ignore it. I am not going to pretend that it did not happen. I am not going to erase your sin with no payment. My justice demands payment!"

The unification bridge between the love of God and the justice of God is His mercy. It is His mercy that stands as a bridge -- a unifying point -- that resolves this great paradox between the love of God and the justness of God. God's justness is satisfied in His mercy. That is why on the cross, Jesus says, "It is finished," rather than, "It is covered." In the Greek language, the phrase "it is finished" is actually one word, *tetelestai*. It means that a task is completed, or a debt is paid in full. It was a business term. It spoke of an indebtedness that was cancelled not due to forgiveness, but due to payment. Always remember, your debt was not just forgiven, your debt was paid. This great love of God and great justness of God seemed pitted against one another. But mercy is the mediator.

The Bible teaches that Jesus redeemed us from our sin. The word "redeemed" means to buy back or to pay a ransom. Too many times Christians think that Jesus paid a ransom to the devil. But that is not accurate. He did not pay some ransom demand to the devil. Jesus did not die to pay the devil anything. He died on the cross to satisfy the justice of God. That is why Isaiah 53 says that it pleased (satisfied) the Father to sacrifice Jesus. Why? Because His justice was satisfied, loosing His love. His mercy bridged the gap and remedied the paradox.

This great mercy of God is celebrated in a Jewish responsive reading that we call Psalm 136. This Psalm was read aloud as a means of reciting God's mercy with the children of Israel. The priests would chant the verse and all the people would respond with the words, "For His mercy endures forever." Remember, they did not have video projectors or song books like we have today. There were no copy machines. All the songs they sang, they sang by memory or responsively. Most often the priests sang the song and the people echoed back either the same words or a responsive phrase. Think about all of Israel standing and singing this song after coming out of the wilderness.

Oh, give thanks to the Lord, for He is good!
    For His mercy endures forever
Oh, give thanks to the God of god's!
    For His mercy endures forever
Oh, give thanks to the Lord of lords!
    For His mercy endures forever
To Him who alone does great wonders,
    For His mercy endures forever
To Him who by wisdom made the heavens,

> For His mercy endures forever
> To Him who laid out the earth above the waters,
> > For His mercy endures forever
> To Him who made great lights,
> > For His mercy endures forever
> The sun to rule by day,
> > For His mercy endures forever
> The moon and stars to rule by night,
> > For His mercy endures forever
> To Him who struck Egypt in their firstborn,
> > For His mercy endures forever
> And brought out Israel from among them,
> > For His mercy endures forever
> With a strong hand and with an outstretched arm,
> > For His mercy endures forever
> To Him who divided the Red Sea in two,
> > For His mercy endures forever
> And made Israel pass through the midst of it,
> > For His mercy endures forever
> But overthrew Pharaoh and his army in the Red Sea,
> > For His mercy endures forever
> To Him who led his people through the wilderness,
> > For His mercy endures forever
> To Him who struck down great kings,
> > For His mercy endures forever
> And gave their land as an inheritance,
> > For His mercy endures forever
> A heritage to Israel His servant,
> > For His mercy endures forever
> Who remembered us in our lowly state,
> > For His mercy endures forever
> And rescued us from our enemies,
> > For His mercy endures forever
> Who gives food to all flesh,
> > For His mercy endures forever
> Oh, give thanks to the God of heaven!
> > For His mercy endures forever

They are rehearsing the mercy of God over and over. Imagine thousands of people singing back to the priests, "For His mercy endures forever!" They understood that they owed their very existence to the mercy of God. God had rescued them by His powerful hand. They had been delivered from the living death of slavery into the freedom of the Promised Land by the mercy of God. This is a theme that is repeated over and over in the Psalms and it is a theme that should be repeated over and over by all of mankind.

Remember from our lesson on sin that one of the meanings of sin is to miss the road. When man missed the road, he separated himself from God. Man's sin creates a great chasm between God and man. This chasm has been portrayed in many different ways over the years, but however it is portrayed, it is a gap; a sin gap. Man's sin creates a breach between God and man. The punishment for man's sin was loss of vital principle. Death was the punishment. This loss of *vital principle* is a breach that is insurmountable from man's perspective. With the loss of vital principle, man lost the power it provides. Man has no power to remove this death sentence. The breach is simply too great.

The only thing that could remove this breach was blood. Sin had caused the breach and the only thing that could satisfy the breach was blood. The Lord tells us in Leviticus 17:11. "For the life of the flesh is in the blood and I have given it to you upon the altar to make atonement for your souls; for it is the blood that makes atonement for the soul." The life of the flesh is in the blood. God told Adam and Eve that if they ate of the Tree of Knowledge, they would surely die. Sin brings death.

When you die you lose life. According to Leviticus 17, the life is in the blood. So, the only thing that can satisfy the sin breach is blood. The writer of Hebrews makes it even more plain. "According to the law almost all things are purified with blood and without the shedding of blood there is no remission of sin" (Hebrews 9:32). It is impossible to forgive sin without the shedding of blood because death is the penalty for sin. This loss of life is required as payment for sin. The life is in the blood. So only blood can make atonement for sin and provide forgiveness.

## MERCY IN THE OLD TESTAMENT

In the Old Testament the concept of mercy is portrayed very graphically in the events that occurred annually on the Day of Atonement. What we call the Day of Atonement is the Jewish festival, Yom Kippur. In the Hebrew language, *kapar* is translated "mercy." Thus, *Yom Kippur*, the Day of Atonement, is the DAY OF MERCY.

So, what happened on that day? What happened on the Day of Mercy? We find the story in Leviticus 16:11-19. As we examine this passage, keep in mind that Aaron was the first High Priest. This position was a generational office that would continue after Aaron died. Future High Priests would be of Aaron's lineage and would take on Aaron's role.

> "And Aaron shall bring the bull of the sin offering, which is for himself and make atonement for himself and for his house and shall kill the bull as the sin offering which is for himself Then he shall take a censer full of burning coals of fire from the altar before the Lord, with his hand s full of sweet incense beaten fine and bring it inside the veil."

So, Aaron takes the coals from the altar and puts them in a censer. He then fills his hands with fine incense. He takes the censer, along with the incense and slips inside the veil. This veil is the veil that separates the Holy Place from the Holy of Holies in the tabernacle. The only thing inside the Holy of Holies is the Ark of the Covenant. He takes the incense in his hands and places it on the coals from the altar that are in the censer. When he does this, a cloud arises as the incense smolders on the hot coals.

It says that he does this lest he die. He has not yet sprinkled the blood on the Mercy Seat, so he must keep himself veiled from the manifest presence of God. God had told Moses that He would dwell between the wings of the cherubim. The cherubim were part of the Mercy Seat and the Mercy Seat was the lid to the Ark of the Covenant. God had told Moses, "You cannot see My face; for no man shall see Me and live" (Exodus 33:20). The incense smoke was necessary to veil Aaron from the manifest presence of God.

The High Priest then sprinkled the blood from the sacrifice on the Mercy Seat seven times. Seven is the number of completeness in the Bible. It speaks of making complete atonement for all sin at that moment. Keep in mind that this is mercy under the Old Covenant and is totally different from what we have now. In the original Hebrew, the word **atonement** really means a covering, or to cover. All that Aaron can do is cover the sin. He has no power to remove the sin. He can only cover it. The Book of Hebrews tells us that the blood of bulls and goats cannot bring forgiveness. It cannot pay the price. All it does is cover the sin until it can be dealt with at a later date. The atonement covers the sin until Jesus dies on the cross and His blood, as the Lamb of God, removes that sin. There on the cross, God deals with sin finally and completely by shedding His blood and paying the debt.

Aaron makes atonement for the sins of Israel by sprinkling the blood on the Mercy Seat. The Mercy Seat is actually the lid to the Ark of the Covenant. It is made of pure gold and has two cherubim fashioned into it. The two cherubim were to be facing one another with their heads bowed and their wings stretched towards one another. It is between the wings of these two cherubim that the manifest presence of God dwelt.

In Exodus 25:22, God told Moses, "I will meet with you and I will speak with you from above the mercy seat, from between the two cherubim." He is saying, "My presence will be right there. If you want to know where I am, you find that Ark of the Covenant and that is where I will be."

At the present time, there is a lot of talk about the end of time. A few years back, the *Left Behind* series sparked a lot of interest about the rapture. Whenever the concept of the rapture comes up, the question is always asked, "How close do you think we are?" There is no doubt that we are close, but there are a couple of things that still must be fulfilled. The main event that we are waiting for is the building of the temple on the temple mount. One of the main reasons for the temple not being built is the absence of the Ark of the Covenant. The Ark of the Covenant disappeared nearly a thousand years ago. We actually have no mention of it after the reign of Josiah and he was killed in somewhere around 609 B.C. Without the Ark of the Covenant the temple really has no focus. If that Ark were to be discovered and returned to Jerusalem, you would find Israel building that temple. It will not matter that there is a mosque on top of that hill and it will not matter how many people come against them. Even if the whole world stands against them, as the Bible prophecies, they will rebuild their temple.

The Ark of the Covenant is detailed in Exodus 25:10-22. In studying the passage, you will notice that the Ark is measured in cubits. A cubit is a rough measurement equal to the distance from the tip of your finger to your elbow, or approximately eighteen inches. Since this distance varies from person to person, the cubit is an approximated measurement. But a cubit is somewhere in the neighborhood of eighteen inches. The Ark of the Covenant consisted of two parts: the box and the lid. The Ark proper is approximately forty-five inches long, twenty-seven inches wide and twenty-seven inches tall. It consists of a bottom and four sides. The lid is the Mercy Seat and covers the open top of the box.

The box of the Ark is constructed of acacia wood and covered in pure gold. Acacia is a small, shrub-like tree that grows in the semi-arid Bible lands. Many times, these trees are almost the only vegetation found in valleys around Sinai. Due to the limited moisture in the region, the trees grow very slowly. This causes the wood to be extremely hard and dense. This density is increased by the fact that the tree deposits waste materials in its heartwood which are preservative in nature. The heartwood is a dark reddish brown, almost ebony color that is beautiful when polished. The density of the wood makes it almost impenetrable by water and the deposits make it unpalatable to insects. For this reason, it is often referred to as an incorruptible wood. It is typological for the box that held God's manifested presence to be constructed of a material that is incorruptible. But this gold plated, incorruptible box was not empty. Hebrews 9:4 lists the

4 Mercy

contents of the Ark as: a golden pot of manna, Aaron's rod that budded and two tablets that are the Ten Commandments.

Each of these three things represents sin and the judgment that followed. All three of these items reminded Israel of a **judgment of God** that had fallen upon the children of God. We find the story of the manna and its accompanying judgment in Numbers 11. Every morning God provided manna for the children of Israel. Every day Israel awakened to find the ground covered with this "bread from heaven." Every morning they gathered a day's supply and this supply sustained them throughout their journey. But in Numbers 11, we find the people murmuring, "I am so tired of manna." Think about what they are really saying -- "I am so tired of what God supplies. I would like something different. I'd like to have a little meat."

To say that God was upset with Israel would be an understatement. He said "How dare you ask for meat? You want meat? I'll give you meat. I'll give you quail." As a matter of fact, God gave them so much quail that the Bible says it came out their nostrils. There is a certain irony in this judgment because He didn't have to punish them with an outside force. He knew their heart. He just played into their gluttonous hearts. He knew their own gluttony -- their own greed -- their own selfishness would kill them. They had been eating manna for an extended period of time and now He gives them meat. They had mounds of quail stacked up for at least a half-mile outside camp. And they ate quail and ate quail and ate quail, until they died of their own gluttony. The manna represents a **judgment of God**.

In Numbers 16 we find the story of the **judgment** tied to Aaron's staff. It is the story of Korah's rebellion. One day, a group of under-leaders came to Moses and Aaron and demanded, "Who made you leader over us? Who said you should be the boss? We are all children of God. We are all equal. We can lead as well as you can." Again, God was upset with their resistance to His plans. God told Moses to tell the people to get away from Korah and these other leaders. Then the earth opened and swallowed up the mutinous leaders, their families and their followers. Then God commanded Moses to secure one staff from each head of the twelve tribes of Israel. The name of each tribe's leader was written on his staff and the staffs were brought into the tabernacle. Aaron's staff was placed with the twelve staffs and all the staffs were left in the tabernacle overnight. God declared that the staff belonging to the man that was the true, God-chosen leader would miraculously produce blossoms overnight. The next morning Aaron's rod had blossomed. Aaron's rod was placed in the Ark as a memorial to the judgment that came upon Korah and the rebellious leaders who opposed God's authority.

Finally, the tablets of the Law represent the **judgment** that came on Israel when the Law was given. While Moses was on the Mountain receiving the Law, Israel fell into idolatry. The judgment for their sin is found in Exodus 32:28. God told Moses to call the Levites and find out who would stand for God. Those who would stand were given the task of purging Israel. On that day, three thousand men were put to death for their idolatry. There is an interesting sidenote here. God always keeps good records. The Bible says that God reconciled us to Himself. Reconciling is a book-keeping term of credits, debits and zero balance. When the Law came, three thousand men died. In Acts 2, the Spirit came, and three thousand men were given life; they were born again. Three thousand men died when the law came and three thousand men gained life when the Spirit came. God reconciled the books.

So, these three items inside the Ark of the Covenant are memorials to the judgment of God. The only thing that separated the people from the judgment of God was the Mercy Seat. That golden lid of the box was the only thing that kept the judgment of God from coming out on the people. The judgment of God was sealed up in that box by the Mercy Seat and the blood was continually applied to the Mercy Seat every year on the Day of Atonement.

## MERCY IN THE NEW TESTAMENT

When we use the term Mercy Seat, we tend to picture a chair. But that is not really what the word means. It literally speaks of a place of mercy or the seat of mercy. When the Old Testament was translated into Greek, a word had to be selected to use for Mercy Seat. The word chosen for the translation is also used in 1 John 2:2. "And He Himself is the propitiation (*mercy seat*) for our sins and not for ours only but also for the whole world." This word propitiation is the same word. It means place of mercy or seat of mercy. Christ is our Mercy Seat. Under the New Covenant, Christ seals up the judgment of God in our life.

This verse is troubling for every person possessing a religious, Pharisaic spirit. It clearly says that Christ is the Mercy Seat for the whole world. Christ has sealed up the judgment of God for the entire world. Anytime you get concerned about the judgment of God, look at that verse. People have said that the AIDs epidemic is the judgment of God against homosexuality, but that cannot be. It is impossible because it is incongruous to Scripture. The Scripture says that He took the sin of the world in His body. It says that He is the place of mercy not only for us but for the whole world. The judgment of God has been set aside until the final Day of Judgment. That is what the Bible tells us. There will be a Day of Judgment, a day of accounting, a day of reckoning. But until that time, the judgment of God is restrained. The judgment of God was satisfied in Christ Jesus on the cross and in His going into hell.

This satisfaction of God's judgment in no way excludes the discipline of God. There is a difference between discipline and judgment. Punishment says you have done something wrong, and you must pay for it. Discipline says you have done something wrong, and your behavior needs to be altered so that it will not happen again. Punishment is about what you have done wrong and paying the price for that wrong. Jesus has already paid the price for your sin and not only yours -- but the sin of the whole world. There will come a day of judgment, but until that day we are all operating in the mercy of God. But the mercy of God does not excuse us from the discipline of the Lord. He disciplines us because He loves us and wants us to walk in His blessings. If we habitually miss the road, the Lord will bring negative reinforcement to bear upon our behavior. This is not punishment, but training in righteousness. It comes because of His great love and mercy.

Jesus is the Mercy Seat of the New Covenant. But unlike the Mercy Seat of the Old Covenant, this Mercy Seat is not sprinkled with the blood of bulls and goats. When God told Moses to construct the Tabernacle and the Ark of the Covenant, He gave specific instructions. He told Moses that he was making an exact replica of what already existed in the heavenlies. Every time the priest sprinkled that blood upon the Mercy Seat it was a prophetic picture. The Book of Hebrews tells us that the heavenly Mercy Seat was sprinkled with the blood of the very Lamb of God when Jesus ascended to the Father. Remember what John the Baptist said when he saw Jesus on the bank of the Jordan River. Israel was looking for the Messiah, the Lord of Lords, the King of kings. They were looking for their rescuer. John could have said, "Behold, the Messiah." Instead, he proclaimed, "Behold the Lamb of God that takes away the sin of the world" (John 1:29). Isn't it amazing that he didn't say "takes away the sin of Israel" or "takes away the sin of the church." He proclaimed that Jesus was the Lamb of God that takes away the sin of the whole world.

Hebrews 9 tells us that Jesus entered the heavenly Holy of Holies with his own blood and forever made redemption for our sin.

> "$_{11}$ But Christ came as High Priest of the good things to come, with the greater and more perfect tabernacle not made with hands, that is, not of this creation. $_{12}$ Not with the blood of goats and calves, but with His own blood He entered the Most Holy Place once for all, having obtained eternal redemption . . . $_{23}$ Therefore it was necessary that the copies of the things in the heavens should be purified with these, but the heavenly things themselves with better sacrifices than these. $_{24}$ for Christ has not entered the holy places made with hands, which are copies of the true, but into heaven itself, now to appear in the presence of God for us."

Remember, the Old Covenant sacrifice did not take away sin — it just covered sin. As a picture of that covering, two goats were utilized on the Day of Atonement: one goat was killed and the other goat was sent into the wilderness as the scapegoat. After atonement had been made in the Holy of Holies, Aaron would go outside of the walls of the tabernacle. He would place his hands on the head of the scapegoat and pronounce that all the sins of Israel for that year were on the head of that goat. The goat was then led out into the wilderness and released. That was a graphic picture of taking away the sins, but it was not permanent. That goat was still out there. He was still roaming around with the sins of Israel on his head. But Jesus, the perfect Lamb of God, did not cover the sin. He took the sin of the entire world in His body and paid the price for those sins.

Hebrews 10 is a wonderful chapter that explains the mercy of God under the New Covenant. The priests of the Old Testament had to repeatedly make the same sacrifices; over and over, day after day. But Jesus made one final and complete sacrifice for sins that ended the sacrificial system. Let's let the text speak for itself.

> 12 But this Man, after He had offered one sacrifice for sins forever, sat down at the right hand of God, 13 from that time waiting till His enemies are made His footstool. 14 For by one offering He has perfected forever those who are being sanctified. 15 But the Holy Spirit also witnesses to us; for after He had said before, 16 "This is the covenant that I will make with them after those days, says the LORD: I will put My laws into their hearts and in their minds I will write them," then He adds, 17 "Their sins and their lawless deeds I will remember no more."

Having made this final and complete sacrifice, Christ sat down at the right hand of God. The Suffering Servant had completed His task as the eternal Lamb of God. He has offered one sacrifice forever and this sacrifice has perfected all those who believe by removing all sin. That sin debt has been paid. As Jesus said on the cross, "It is finished."

This is the mercy of the New Covenant. Christ took our sin in His body on the cross. He died for those sins and went into hell for those sins. He paid the full price of judgment for us. By the mercy of God, our sins have been dealt with and God remembers them no more. That is why we can know for certain that 1John 1:9 is not for the believer. If it were meant for the believer, you would be confessing something to Him that He has removed from His mind and remembers no more. 1 John 1:9 says, "If we confess our sins, He is faithful and just to forgive us our sins and to cleanse us from all unrighteousness." This verse is not for the child of God. It is a portrayal of what is necessary for salvation. When we first come to Jesus, we confess our sins. He cleanses us of our sins. Notice that it says that He is faithful and just to forgive us. Jesus was condemned for our sin. It would be **unjust** to hold us accountable for that which Jesus has already paid. Justice demands our forgiveness because Christ has already paid our debt. When we confess our sin, His mercy satisfies His justice and releases His love.

Because of this great act of Mercy, we have "boldness to enter the Holiest *(Holy of Holies)* by the blood of Jesus, by a new and living way which He consecrated for us, through the veil, that is, His flesh. Let us draw near in full assurance of faith" (Hebrews 10:19 emphasis added). We have this boldness because we have been cleansed from our sin. Our sin has been removed and God does not even remember it. The blood of Jesus dealt with our sin, and we are perfectly clean before our Father God. There is no sin in us. "But if we walk in the light as He is in the light, we have fellowship with one another, and the blood of Jesus Christ His Son cleanses us from all sin" (1 John 1:7).

If sin remained in us or if our cleansing was conditional upon our confessing, we could never have boldness to enter the throne room. We would always be wondering if we forgot to confess some sin. Every time we came before God, we would wonder whether He was going to mention some sin that we had forgotten to confess. No! To enter with boldness, we must be assured that we have been cleansed from our sin and there is no chance our wrongful acts will ever be brought back up again. That is the mercy of God.

Christ cleansed us by taking our sin in His body on the tree and then taking His blood into the heavenly Holy of Holies to pay for that sin. At that heavenly altar, He sprinkled the blood of the Lamb of God, His own precious blood, upon the Mercy Seat of God. You may remember that after the resurrection of Jesus, Mary tried to touch Jesus and He told her not to do so. He said, "Do no touch me for I have not yet ascended to the Father" (John 20:17). He is speaking of His role as High Priest. After the High Priest had taken the blood from the altar, He could not be touched by any human until He offered that blood upon the mercy seat. If he was touched by anyone, he was defiled and had to go back to the sacrificial altar and start the whole process again. On the cross, Jesus was sacrificed as the Lamb of God and as the eternal High Priest, He collected His own blood. Jesus was then sent into hell itself for three days, where he paid the penalty for our sin. The moment that debt was paid, He was released. That is what Paul is referring to in Romans 4:25, when he tells us that Christ was "delivered up because of our offenses and was raised because of our justification." He was raised because of our justification; not for our justification. When the debt was paid, we were justified. It was as though we had never sinned. Our sin was removed. At the very moment of our justification, the justice of God demanded that Christ be released. For Him to have remained in hell one moment after our debt was paid would have been an injustice. He was raised **because** our justification was complete.

When He appears to Mary, He is on the way to being restored to His eternal position at the right hand of the Father. But before He ascends to heaven, He reassures His disciples by appearing to Mary. According to Hebrews, He is carrying His own blood for the sanctification of the heavenly mercy seat. He tells Mary "Don't touch me right now, I have not yet ascended." A few verses later, we find Him saying to Thomas "Touch my hands, put your hand in the hole in my side" (John 20:27). He is willing to allow Thomas to touch Him. What has changed? Apparently, in the interval between these two appearances He has been to the Mercy Seat. He has sprinkled His blood in the Holy of Holies and secured our eternal forgiveness. His mercy has bridged the gap between the perfect justice of God and the perfect love of God. Christ bridged that gap and opened the way for God's love to flow out into the world. God is love and His mercy endures forever!

# CHAPTER 5

# GRACE

*For grace is given not because we have done good works, but in order that we may be able to do them.*
Augustine

In the mid 1700's, the Great Awakening was sweeping back and forth across the Atlantic. The mighty hand of God was changing the United States and Great Britain. But this massive move of the Holy Spirit had little effect upon John Newton. John was the captain of his own slave ship. Black slaves were collected in West Africa and transported to the West Indies and America. There they were sold mainly to work on the huge plantations of the New World. Trading in human souls makes one a cold man.

John Newton lived a cruel and brutal life and his heart was dead. But on a voyage back to England everything changed. The ship was being assaulted by an unusually vicious storm and it looked as though all would be lost. Newton began reading Thomas a Kempis' classic book, *The Imitation of Christ,* and was touched by the amazing grace of God. His life began to change. He sold his ship and became an adamant crusader against slavery. It is interesting to note that the British Parliament banished slavery throughout its empire in the very year that Newton died. After leaving the sea, he became pastor of an Anglican Church in Olney, England. While there he began to write hymns. The most famous of these is his personal testimony of God's amazing grace.

> Amazing Grace, how sweet the sound
> That saved a wretch like me
> I once was lost but now I'm found
> Was blind but now I see.
>
> 'Twas grace that taught my heart to fear
> And grace my fears relieved;
> How precious did that grace appear
> The hour I first believed.
>
> Thro' many dangers, toils and snares,
> I have already come;
> 'Tis grace hath brought me safe thus far,
> And grace will lead me home
>
> The Lord has promised good to me,
> His Word my hope secures;
> He will my shield and portion be,
> As long as life endures.
>
> When we've been there ten thousand years,
> Bright shining as the sun;
> We've no less days to sing God's praise,
> Than when we first begun.

Indeed, there is nothing more amazing than God's amazing grace. In the church world today, there is much talk about grace. It has become the "buzz word" over the last few years. But the word is being given such generic use that it is hard to know what is really meant by grace. In the last lesson, we looked at the love of God and His infinite mercy. But beyond love and mercy, there is grace. Even though people tend to use the word grace when they really mean mercy, there is a distinct difference between mercy and grace in the Bible. Although love, mercy and grace are intricately linked together, they are quite distinct.

In the second chapter of Ephesians, Paul graphically displays the interrelationship of these concepts when he says, "But God, who is rich in mercy, because of His great love with which He loved us, even when we were dead in trespasses, made us alive together with Christ (by grace you have been saved ) and raised us up together and made us sit together in the heavenly places in Christ Jesus, that in the ages to come He might show the exceeding riches of His grace in His kindness toward us in Christ Jesus." We are saved by grace because of God's great love manifested through his wonderful mercy. By His mercy, our sins are dealt with and by His grace we are seated in heavenly places. We will deal with this truth in more detail later but notice that this verse says that He made us sit together in heavenly places. This is a past tense verb. This event has already occurred. It is not that God is going to seat us in heavenly places in the future. This event has already occurred. It is past tense. By His grace we are NOW seated in heavenly places.

Traditionally, we have defined mercy and grace with a little memory device. We have said that Mercy is NOT GETTING what you DO DESERVE, and that Grace is GETTING what you DO NOT deserve. So, mercy is averting a negative and grace is gaining a positive. We also often hear that grace is UNMERITED FAVOR. And although all these definitions are true, grace is much more complex than any of these.

## SO, WHAT IS GRACE?

Since the New Testament was originally written in Greek, we may be able to gain some insight by examining the meaning of the word we translate grace. The Greek word is the word *xaris* and the root of this word is *xairo*. *Xairo* means to rejoice, be glad, be joyful, or to be full of joy. *Xaris* means that which bestows or occasions this joy, pleasure or delight. *Xaris* speaks of a beneficial opportunity or generous gift.

It is difficult for some to understand grace because they have a distorted view of God and His presence. Because they view God as austere and fearful, they have trouble understanding grace as a generous gift from God that bestows joy and pleasure. But Psalm 16:11 gives us a different perspective on the presence of God. David says, "You will show me the path of life; in Your presence is fullness of joy; at Your right hand are pleasures forevermore." This is quite a contrast to the traditional view of God and His presence. Think about this verse with the meaning of the

Greek word *Xaris*. Grace is that which provides pleasure or delight and in His presence is the fullness of joy and pleasure forevermore. *Xaris* is about God delighting in us.

Since God is God and knows no limit, He can do whatever He pleases. King David understood that a king does not have to tolerate those things that displease him. He can banish those things that bring displeasure or replace them with things that please him. He is King and he can do whatever he pleases. That is what he expresses when he says, "But our God is in heaven; he does whatever He pleases" (Psalm 115:3). God is King of all and He does whatever He pleases. If there is joy in His presence and He only does the things that please Him, then He is not going to do things that displease Him. Psalm 135:6 reiterates this idea when it says, "Whatever the LORD pleases He does, in heaven and in earth, in the seas and in all deep places."

He is King and He only does the things that bring Him joy. Psalm 16:3 clearly portrays what gives God pleasure. "As for the saints who are on the earth, 'They are the excellent ones, in whom is all my delight.'" As New Covenant believers, we are His saints. He calls us the excellent ones, in whom is all His delight. In the presence of the Lord, there is fullness of joy and pleasures forevermore. He only does what He pleases. He calls us His delight.

So, let us put this all together: God has all power and does what He desires; He only does the things that please Him and He says we are what pleases Him. That opens us up for all kinds of blessings.

Isaiah 53:10 says that it "pleased the Father" to bruise Jesus." As hard as it is for us to comprehend, it pleased the Father for Jesus to die on the cross. And Hebrews 12:2 tells us that Jesus "suffered the cross for the joy that was set before Him." His joy and the Father's grand pleasure is in seeing His grace at work, bringing people into the Kingdom and bestowing His blessings upon them.

When we move into the New Testament, these things are even more specifically addressed. "But as it is written: 'Eye has not seen, nor ear heard, nor have entered into the heart of man the things which God has prepared for those who love Him" (1 Corinthians 2:9). We cannot even imagine the good things that flow from the joyful, pleasurable presence of God. James, the brother of Jesus, encouraged the early church with this promise: "Every good gift and every perfect gift is from above and comes down from the Father of lights, with whom there is no variation or shadow of turning" (James 1:17). If we are His delight, then delighting us brings Him the most joy. Now, that is incongruous to most people's thinking. Most people grow up thinking that their job is to somehow please God by making some great sacrifice for Him. But His delight is not in our sacrifice. His delight is in giving good things to us. His grace is what provides the avenue for those blessings.

In the last few pages of the Old Testament, we find the prophecies of Zephaniah. The prophet speaks of the wickedness of Israel and judgment that is coming. But he foretells of a remnant of faithful believers who will receive the promise of God. And according to the apostle, Paul, we who are of faith are that remnant. In the closing words of Zephaniah's prophecy, we find a phenomenal promise. He says, "The LORD your God in your midst, the Mighty One, will save; he will rejoice over you with gladness, he will quiet you with His love, he will rejoice over you with singing" (Zephaniah 3:17). Can you imagine that? God, the creator of the universe, singing over us. We are always trying to sing to God, and yet, He is singing to us! He rejoices over us. In Hebrew, the word "rejoice" means to twirl around joyfully. When God thinks about you, He jumps up off His throne, twirls around and says, "Yeah!" You are the delight of God. This is not because of anything you have done. You are His delight because of who you are in Christ.

A truth that will be developed thoroughly in Book 3 is that love demands expression. The greatest joy we experience is in giving gifts to those we love. Because of the great love God has for us, His great delight is in giving to us. He delights in us. Adam and Eve made the wrong choice and missed the opportunity for God to fully delight in man. They chose the wrong tree. They lost that vital principle called life and brought in sin. They made mercy, repentance, and forgiveness necessary. But because of His great love for us, God goes beyond the mercy and forgiveness. He extends grace to us.

The mercy of God dealt with our old man and our sin. In his first letter to the church, Peter says that "Christ bore our sins in His own body on the tree" (1 Peter 2:24). On the cross, Jesus took all the sin of all mankind into His body. The sky grew dark as the evil of all generations came rushing into Jesus. All the sins of the past came rushing forward in time. All the sins of the present came crushing in. All the sins of the future — sins that had not even been committed yet — hammered into Christ's body. He took all the sin of all mankind. But He went even further than simply taking the sins in His body. He actually became Sin. 2 Corinthians 5:21 says, "For He made Him who knew no sin to be sin for us." The sinless, spotless Lamb of God became sin so that Sin and its power might die. God did not wait for us. He did not demand that we get our lives in order that we might receive the blessing of God. No! "God demonstrates His own love toward us, in that while we were still sinners, Christ died for us" (Romans 5:8).

Because of His great love, He wants to bless us. It is His delight to bless us, but our sin prohibited that blessing. His mercy removed that hindrance to our blessing and secured the way for the grace of God to be poured out on us. His grace deals with our new man. When a person places his faith in Christ for salvation, he appropriates the work that the mercy of God has provided and becomes a totally new creation. He is no longer like Adam in that all his sins have been forgiven. Even those sins that are in the future are dealt with. Christ took them in His body. Therefore, it is impossible for him to be a sinner. His sin has been removed. He is a new, righteous creation.

That is what Paul is talking about in 2 Corinthians 5:17. "Therefore, if anyone is in Christ, he is a new creation; old things have passed away; behold, all things have become new." We are not just forgiven. We are a totally new creature. That is what is meant by being Born Again. We are no longer merely human. We are the righteousness of God in Christ Jesus. Paul explains it this way, "For He made Him who knew no sin to be sin for us, that we might become the righteousness of God in Him" (2 Corinthians 5;21). As surely as Christ became our sin, we became His righteousness. He became sin that we might become righteous. We made an exchange — sin for righteousness. His mercy forgave sin. His grace made us righteous.

The word righteous means to be in right-standing with God. Before God could delight in us, we had to be in right-standing with Him. He had to make you righteous, so that He could delight in you again. You had separated yourself from Him. You had separated yourself from His blessing. You had missed the road. God had to make a way back. As noted earlier, the Scriptures tell us that He is God, and He does whatever He pleases. He wanted to delight in us, and we had destroyed that relationship. His grace restores that relationship and secures the way for the blessing. God went to a lot of trouble to restore His delight in blessing us. But over the years the church has gone to a lot of trouble to make it difficult to get that blessing.

The mercy of God dealt with our old man by putting it to death on the cross with Jesus. Grace deals with the new man by making us whole. Ephesians 2:5 says that "by His grace we are saved." When most people talk about being saved, they are talking about mercy. They are really saying, "I once was a sinner and Jesus forgave me of my sin." When we ask someone if they are saved, we usually mean, "Are you going to heaven when you die?" But the word "saved" is the Greek word *sodzo*, which means to be made whole. Our sin and our sinful nature have left us in a "dead" state. Ephesians 2:1 says that "while we were still dead in our trespasses and sin, He made us alive." When we are in sin, we are living in a less than intended place; a place that God did not intend. We missed the road, and we are operating at this less than intended level. By His grace, He comes into that dead place and makes us alive. He brings us back into a place of intended purpose.

Your intended purpose is to bring glory to God. You bring glory to God by allowing Him to bless you. In John 15, Jesus states that He is the vine and we are the branches. If we abide in

Him, we bear fruit. It is not our fruit; it is His fruit. He is the vine. It is His life forces flowing through us that produce His fruit. That is why John 15:8 says, "By this My Father is glorified, that you bear much fruit." It is His fruit and His fruit in our life brings Him glory. It is for this reason that He resists the proud and exalts the humble. It takes humility to say, "It is not me. I am just on the receiving end." Our pride wants to say, "I did this and that for the Lord." But in reality, we didn't do it. He did it. It is His fruit. We should serve God out of gratitude, rather than obligation. We should serve Him because we enjoy His delight so much that we cannot imagine not walking with Him.

Obedience is nothing more than walking with the Lord. It is not keeping laws and regulations. If God tells you to go somewhere, you know that is where you are going to be blessed. It may not always be easy to do what He says and go where He says to go. But there is one thing you can know; there is great blessing in that difficult place. Obedience is necessary in order to stay in the center of His blessing. Sin is missing the road to that blessing. His grace makes us whole so that we have the ability to walk in the blessings.

## GRACE GIVES US MERIT

His grace restored what was lost and made us whole. Jesus said that He "came to seek and save that which was lost" (Luke 19:10). He did not say that He came to seek and save those who were lost. Man lost his intended purpose and the vital principle that God had designed for him. God's grace restores that vital principle in us and makes us whole, so that we can live out our intended purpose. That which is lost in sin is restored in grace.

The grace of God restores that which was lost and gives us merit before God. The value of a product is determined by what is paid for the object. When you buy a diamond, it is given an appraised value. But the appraised value is not the real value. The jeweler may present you with a certificate that states that the diamond is worth three thousand dollars. But if you tell him that you would like to sell him the diamond, he will not pay you anything close to three thousand dollars. What he is willing to pay for the diamond is really the worth of the diamond. Your worth is determined by what price has been paid for you or what someone is willing to pay for you.

Many Christians journey through life with a feeling of unworthiness. When they pray, they approach God as one unworthy to be in His presence. But this is not Biblical. That is false humility and is an insult to the grace of God. You are valuable and of great worth. Your worth is established by the price God paid for you -- the blood of His own son, Jesus. You were not redeemed with corruptible things, like silver or gold . . . "but with the precious blood of Christ" (1 Peter 1:18-19). Our value and position before God has been restored.

Our right-standing before God is not based upon our own personal righteousness. The prophet tells us that our greatest works of righteousness are but "filthy rags" before God (Isaiah 54:6). Our right-standing, our merit before God, is by way of an exchange. We traded our sin for Christ's righteousness. Because of this exchange, we stand in the righteousness of Christ. The apostle Paul clearly understood this fact. He proclaimed that he exchanged everything, that he might gain Christ and be found in Him, not having his "own righteousness, which is from the law, but that which is through faith in Christ, the righteousness which is from God by faith" (Philippians 3:9). Our righteousness is a righteousness of faith. We apply our faith to what God has already accomplished. We must simply have faith in what Christ has fulfilled. But according to Ephesians 2:8 even the faith required is given to us as a gift of God. It is as though Father God gave one requirement for salvation – believe. But He knew that we were incapable of supplying that faith on our own, so He gave us the measure of faith that He Himself required. Because of this gift of faith-righteousness, we have the right to receive the blessings. Through this exchange, we have been given the spirit of adoption and we are now joint-heirs with Jesus Christ.

We have been adopted into the family of God and we are heirs of God. One of the most famous verses in the Bible states this very succinctly, "Behold what manner of love the Father has bestowed on us, that we should be called children of God" (1 John

3:1). That is what we mean when we talk about righteousness. Righteousness is our position as a child of God through the exchanged life we have in Christ. Many tend to make righteousness a fulfillment of the law. But that will never make us righteous. If we could obtain right-standing by keeping the law, there was no reason for Christ to die. New Testament righteousness says that I am placed in right-standing with God, so that the blessings of God can be released. My life reflects that blessing as I walk in right-standing with the Father. That walk of blessing clearly reflects the goodness and lovingkindness of God. It is walking right because I am right with God. That is righteousness. Right-walking coming out of our right-standing. Righteousness does not come by keeping the law.

We keep the Law because we are righteous, and we want to walk in that righteousness. The law was given to show man where he was missing the blessing of God. For example, God gives us six days to labor and one day of rest. He knows how we are designed. We need a day of rest to unwind and retool. We are not designed to labor seven days a week. If we work seven days, we quickly discover that our productivity lessens. God designed us for six days of labor and one day of rest. When we violate that design, we limit the blessing of the Designer. Our righteousness is the work of His grace in us. He gives us right-standing so that His blessings can flow in us and through us. Because of this right-standing we have a right to expect the blessings of God in our life.

## HIS GRACE PROVIDES FAVOR

His grace provides not only merit but favor as well. Many of us have a difficult time accepting the fact that we have a right to expect God to bless us. We have a tendency to come at it from a mercy standpoint that says, "I don't really deserve it, but I'm getting it anyway." While that sounds spiritual, it is not Biblically sound. We are deserving because Christ made us worthy. We deserve the blessings of God because Christ has given us right-standing before God. It takes humility to say that we deserve the blessings of God. False humility says, "I am not worthy." If you are not worthy, Jesus died in vain. He died to make you worthy. Righteousness says, "I not only receive these blessings, I have a right to them." He tells us to come as little children. Until you understand that you have a right to His blessings, you will never come as a little child, and you will never appropriate true faith.

Right before His death, Jesus spent time praying in the Garden of Gethsemane. There He prayed for His disciples. Then He prayed, "I do not pray for these alone, but also for those who will believe in Me through their word" (John 17:20). One day as I read those words, revelation burst through – He is praying for me. I believed because of their word. My faith in Jesus is based upon the testimony of these apostles and leaders. In those last few hours of His life, He took time to pray for us. What He prayed next is life changing. "And the glory which You gave Me I have given them, that they may be one just as We are one" (John 17:21). He has not only forgiven our sin and given us His righteousness, but He has also given us His glory.

This glory He has given us is phenomenal. It is the very glory that the Father gave Him. The Amplified Bible does an excellent job of exposing us to the true depth of this glory in John 1:14. "And the Word (Christ) became flesh (human, incarnate) and tabernacled (fixed His tent of flesh, lived awhile) among us; and we [actually] saw His glory (His honor, His majesty), such glory as an only begotten son receives from his father, full of grace (favor, loving-kindness) and truth." The favor and loving-kindness that a father bestows upon His only son has been given to us. This is the glory that Jesus gave us. Grace provided this same glory for us. God lavishes favor and loving-kindness upon us as if we were His only begotten Son. No wonder Paul exclaims that we are "joint-heirs with Christ" (Romans 8:17). He has given us the glory that the Father gave Him.

It is sad that so many believers miss out on the liberating nature of this truth. Because they never realize what Christ has done, they live their life in hope rather than true faith. For instance, when people pray for healing, most often they do so not in faith, but in hope. They are not convinced that they have a right to healing. They do not understand that Christ purchased that right for them. They simply pray and hope that God answers their prayer. When we receive revelation of the glory that has been given to us, we pray from a position of expectation rather than hope. Our understanding of our glorified position in Christ creates a boldness of faith. This boldness is based upon who we are in Christ, seated at the right hand of the Father. Our faith works and we have the things that we ask because we have the same favor as the only begotten Son of God.

Because of His great love for us, He desires to open the windows of heaven and pour out His blessings on us. This has been in His heart all along. When Israel was entering the Promised Land, they passed through a valley between two hills. On one side the priests proclaimed the curses that would be on them if they did not obey the voice of the Lord. On the opposing hill, priests proclaimed the blessings that would come if they obeyed the voice of the Lord.

Listen to these words of blessing that the priests spoke:

"If you fully obey the Lord your God and carefully keep all his commands that I am giving you today, the Lord your God will set you high above all the nations of the world. You will experience all these blessings if you obey the Lord your God: Your towns and your fields will be blessed. Your children and your crops will be blessed. The offspring of your herds and flocks will be blessed. Your fruit baskets and breadboards will be blessed. Wherever you go and whatever you do, you will be blessed. The Lord will conquer your enemies when they attack you. They will attack you from one direction, but they will scatter from you in seven! The Lord will guarantee a blessing on everything you do and will fill your storehouses with grain. The Lord your God will bless you in the land he is giving you. If you obey the commands of the Lord your God and walk in his ways, the Lord will establish you as his holy people as he swore he would do. Then all the nations of the world will see that you are a people claimed by the Lord and they will stand in awe of you" (Deuteronomy 28:1-10).

This favor brings a glory to our life that causes the world to stand in awe. But even as God proclaimed these blessings over Israel, He knew man's hearts. Man would never fully obey the voice of the Lord and open up the avenue of blessing. He understood that Sin would always be a blockage to that flow. That blockage had to be removed to allow His blessings to flow. The cross was no after-thought. It was understood from the beginning (Revelation 13:8). That sin blockage was removed as Jesus became Sin for us. Justification makes it as though sin was never there. Jesus has taken it away. He has taken my sin, removed it as far as the east is from the west and remembers it no more. He does not tell us, "You better act right, because I died on the cross for you." That is manipulation and religion; that is not God. God says, "It is as if you had never sinned. You are free!"

There is an old song that says, "He paid a debt He did not owe; I owed a debt I could not pay." You could not pay it and you can never pay it. So quit wallowing there - that is nothing more than misplaced pride. Pride refuses to accept the free gift of God's grace. Pride says, "It is my debt, and I must repay the one who paid my debt." But that kind of thinking leads to religious bondage. True humility says, "I am free! My sins have been removed, so I am sinless." Many people talk about being free from sin and yet, are still sin conscious. When you are free from sin, you are as free as if you had never committed a sin. We serve God because we love Him and because of the blessings He has placed in our life -- not because we have some debt to pay. If you serve God out of debt, you will burn out.

Legalism teaches that your righteousness is dependent upon your obedience. If you do the right things, you are righteous. But as we have seen, the truth is quite opposite. You are righteous, so therefore you do the right things. In the same way that your sin does not make you a sinner: you were born a sinner with a sin nature and therefore you sinned. When you were Born Again, you were given a righteous nature. Therefore, your righteousness causes you to do the right things.

Anyone who operates in legalism operates in fear. I did it for years. I even preached it for years and put fear on people. I had great response to altar calls because I could manipulate and play on people's emotions. I could make people feel lower than a snake's belly. Then when it came time for invitation and we sang,

"Just As I Am." People gave their life to Jesus just one more time. But that is not right. That is bondage and fear.

We did not receive the spirit of bondage that leads to fear. In Romans 8:15, Paul says, "You did not receive the spirit of bondage again to fear, but you received the Spirit of adoption by whom we cry out, 'Abba, Father.' The Spirit Himself bears witness with our spirit that we are children of God and if children, then heirs-- heirs of God and joint heirs with Christ, if indeed we suffer with Him, that we may also be glorified together." We have received the Spirit of adoption, but not a worldly type of adoption. We have received a spiritual adoption wherein we are intrinsically changed.

This adoption brings with it the glory of being a child of God. This adoption brings with it the merit or worthiness of being a child of God. This adoption brings us into a place of favor and blessing as a child of God. This wonderful, never-ending, all-sufficient grace of God is all we need.

## HOW DO WE ACCESS THIS GREAT GRACE?

In order for grace to be grace, you cannot earn it. If you must do something to earn the blessings, it is not grace but wages. "Now to him who works, the wages are not counted as grace but as debt" (Romans 4:4). No matter what you try to offer, you cannot pay for grace. There is no price on grace. The price has been paid by another. Paul calls it the "gift of grace" (1 Timothy 4:14).

To receive a gift, all you must do is receive. If you want to receive a gift, you first must believe the gift is for you. If someone wanted to give you a thousand dollars, it would do you no good unless you had faith that the person actually had the funds. You would have to believe the person was financially capable of giving such a gift. Not only that, but you would have to believe that the person really wanted to give the money to you. The same is true of God's grace.

Within a span of a few verses, Paul twice tells us that "by faith we have access into grace" (Romans 4:16; 5:2). We must believe that because of His great love and mercy He has justified us. He has taken our sin and now it is as though we had never sinned. Then by His grace He glorifies us as His son providing both merit and favor to us. Israel never fully entered in the rest of grace. Hebrews 3:19 says that they could not "enter in because of unbelief." We must apply our faith to this grace that has been poured out for us and walk in the abundant blessings of God.

# CHAPTER 6

# EMPOWERMENT

*We should therefore learn that the only good we have is what the Lord has given us gratuitously; that the only good we do is what He does in us; that it is not that we do nothing ourselves, but that we act only when we have been acted upon, in other words under the direction and influence of the Holy Spirit.*
John Calvin

In the last chapter, we learned that grace empowers us to live the life that God intended for man to live. Through His grace we are empowered to live the "I CAN" life. This empowerment does not come by some wave of a magic wand. Our empowerment is a process, and we now turn our attention to that process. As we enter this last chapter on the foundation principles, my prayer for you is that which Paul uttered for the saints in Ephesus. "Father of glory, may give to you the spirit of wisdom and revelation in the knowledge of Him, the eyes of your understanding being enlightened; that you may know what is the hope of His calling, what are the riches of the glory of His inheri-tance in the saints and what is the exceeding greatness of His power toward us who believe, according to the working of His mighty power" (Ephesians 1:17-19).

We have an inheritance in Christ, and it is our responsibility to possess that inheritance. This inheritance is more just going to heaven when we die. It is enjoying the kingdom of heaven while we live. An inheritance is provided at the death of the benefactor. Our inheritance was provided when Christ died. It is now our responsibility to claim what is ours. We have inherited the "divine nature" (2 Peter 1:4), and He has empowered us to walk out that nature.

## JUSTIFICATION

The first step in the process of our empowerment is our justification. Justification is the process by which sinful man is made acceptable to Holy God. It is the process wherein God makes us acceptable and holy. God's desire is to take sinful man and return him to the place of purity he had in the Garden of Eden. God wants to restore us to that place of relationship and power that man had before sin entered the scene. Justification is not simply forgiveness. Justification is eradication of sin to the point where there is no longer even the memory of sin. Justification takes us to a place where it is as though we have never even sinned. He restores purity to us.

Many Christians walk around with no clear understanding of justification. They believe that they are simply a sinner saved by grace. As long as you believe and confess that you are just a sinner saved by grace, you have not realized your justification. It has never become real to you. God has proclaimed that you are saved and justified. But you keep saying, "I am just a sinner saved by grace." If you still feel that way, then sin with its memory and scars has not been removed. If justification takes us to a place where it is as though we have never sinned, then we are not just sinners saved by grace; we are saints. We do not talk about our sin, because we are as pure as we would be if we had never sinned. If we never sinned, we would have no sin to talk about.

I John 1:9 says, "If we confess our sins, He is faithful and just to forgive us our sins and to cleanse us from all unrighteousness." As we have said, this verse was not intended to be the sacrificial altar of the New Covenant. It is a verse explaining the process of justification. When we confess our sins, He forgives us and cleanses us from ALL unrighteousness. It is a done deal.

When we come to Christ, we confess our sinful state. He then forgives all our sins and cleanses us of all unrighteousness. He makes us as clean as we would be if we had never sinned. If you believe that you must rehearse your sins to God before He can forgive you, you will never walk in justification. You are continually trying to remind God and yourself that you have sinned. But He has placed all your sin upon Jesus. Thus removing even the trace of sin from you.

**Justification And Grace**

Justification is God's declaration that the demands of His Law have been fulfilled in the righteousness of His Son. The basis for this declaration is the death of Christ. Romans 5:9 tells us that we have been "justified by His blood" and Hebrews 10:14 says that "we are perfected forever by the sacrificial death of Christ." We are perfected forever because all our sin has been removed. If all our sin is removed from us, then all that is left is purity. We are sinless because Christ took our sin in His body on the tree and satisfied justice for us.

Justice is satisfied when the required penalty is paid. Jesus went into hell to satisfy the justice of God by paying the penalty for our sins. When that justice was satisfied, He was resurrected. According to Romans 4:25, Jesus "was delivered up because of our offenses and was raised because of our justification." Take note of the fact that this verse does not say that Jesus was raised FOR our justification. It says that He was raised BECAUSE of our justification. In that regard, our justification caused His liberation and resurrection.

When we are justified, it is just as if we had never sinned. When we come to that place, we are justified. Once the penalty is paid, we are justified. Jesus can no longer stay in hell because there is nothing left for Him to pay. He is released because our sin debt has been paid and we are justified. At a particular point in Jesus' payment, God the Father, the Eternal Judge, said, "Enough! It is paid!" At that very moment, we were justified, and Jesus had to be released. Once a man in prison has paid his debt to society, he is released. To keep him any longer would not be justice. To keep Jesus in hell after our justification would not be justice.

It is our teaching of justification by grace that sets Christianity apart from all other religions. No other religion teaches justification by grace. All the other religions of the world teach justification by works. They believe that they are justified by what they do. Only Christianity says, "We are not justified by what we do, but by what Christ did." There is nothing we can do to justify ourselves. The Scripture says that no man is justified by the works of the law. "For all have sinned and fall short of the glory of God, being justified freely by His grace through the redemption that is in Christ Jesus. God has intended for His glory to be our glory" (Romans 3:23-24). He desired to put His glory on us, but our sin kept us out of that glory. So, Jesus justified us. This justification puts us in a position wherein we can receive the glory. If Jesus is glorified and He comes into us, then we are glorified. But we can never attain this glory through our own works. We receive it through the justification by grace.

When God justifies us, two things occur. He charges our sin to Christ, and He credits Christ's righteousness to us. That is exactly what Paul says in 2 Corinthians 5:21. "For He made Him who knew no sin to be sin for us, that we might become the righteousness of God in Him." The first step in justification occurred when God put our sin on Jesus. The second step occurred when He credited Christ's righteousness to our account. In the book of Romans, this is referred to as reckoning. He tells us to "reckon ourselves to be dead to sin" (Romans 6:11). He is using accounting terms. He took your sin and moved it from your liability column to Jesus' liability column. He took Christ's righteousness out of His asset column and put it in your asset column. That is what occurs in justification. Our sin is removed, and Christ's righteousness is credited to our account.

This is what the apostle Paul is referring to in Roman 5:18. "Through one Man's righteous act, the free gift came to all men, resulting in justification of life." This righteousness is complete because it is the righteousness of God apart from the Law. When man tries to make himself righteous and justify himself, he is never completely successful. He may be better and improved, but he is never perfect. Even if one could become perfect at some point in time, there is still the glaring sin of the past that demands attention. Man, in his religions goes through all sorts of rituals trying to justify himself and make himself complete. It never works. Only God's justification by grace can make man complete. Our righteousness is complete in that it justifies us from all things. "And by Him everyone who believes is justified from all things from which you could not be justified by the law of Moses" (Acts 13:35). The Law of Moses could not do it. The Law can never justify you. All the Law can do is condemn you by revealing how fully you have fallen short of the glory. You cannot arrive at perfection through your own works. Our only hope of justification is by the grace of God. Justification through grace is God's part, but faith in that justification is our part.

## Justification And Faith

We access this grace justification in the same way we access everything God has provided for us. We access our justification by faith. Romans 4:16 and 5:2 make that very clear. Our faith is the key that accesses our justification. All we must do is believe Christ has justified us and then accept that justification. "Therefore, we conclude that a man is justified by faith apart from the deeds of the law" (Romans 3:28). You must work hard to confuse the meaning of that verse. Yet, the church and cults alike have complicated it for years. We are justified by faith. It is apart from the law or any works we might do. The Scriptures are clear, we access the justification by grace by our faith.

By grace, God justified us. But not only did He justify us, He justified all man. The Scripture says that He took the sin of the world in His body. That is what grace provides, but grace alone is not sufficient. It requires faith to activate the grace. By faith, we have access into this grace. It is of faith that it might be according to grace. God paid the price to justify all men, but all mankind will not access that justification. It is not by our works; it is by our faith.

The world has a real problem accepting Christianity because it requires the humility of faith to receive the promises of God. No amount of work can secure them, only the simple faith of acceptance. Religion always bases blessing and salvation upon man's works. This gives man something in which to boast -- something in which to take pride. But Christianity boasts in the fact that Christ did it all and our greatest deeds are but filthy rags before Him. Islam has a real problem with Christians. The problem is that we do not have to do anything for our salvation except believe and that bothers them. They call us lazy, slothful sluggards. Although that may sometimes be true, the truth is that there is nothing that we can do to save ourselves. All of our Meccas and kneeling and praying five times a day and chanting mantras and doing all sorts of works of righteousness will never justify us. We are only justified when we humble ourselves and say, "Lord God, there is nothing I can do but accept what you have done." That is why God says that He exalts the humble but resists the proud.

In God's accounting system, faith counts as righteousness. Abraham is used as an example of this faith-righteousness in Romans 4. Paul says that Abraham's faith was accounted to him as righteousness. You believe and God counts it as a work of righteousness. When you believe, God records that in His books as righteousness. Only our faith is pure. All our works are tainted by this world. But our faith is a gift of God and flows from the spirit realm, in and through us and back into the spirit realm. The only righteous thing we can do is believe. Think about the fact that all sin is unbelief at its core. If sin is unbelief, then faith is the only thing that is righteous. Faith is "unsin" since "whatever is not from faith is sin" (Romans 14:23).

As one who has been justified, sanctified and glorified (Romans 8:29-30), it is impossible for you to act unrighteously. As long as you believe, anything you do is counted as righteous. This is what Paul is addressing in Romans 7:20. He says that when he sins, "It is no longer I who do it, but sin that dwells in me." He goes on to say that he is at war with the members of his body. Every time he sins, the real Paul is saying, "Don't do that!"

Because the real Paul is the spirit man, Paul, and that man is seated in heavenly places in Christ Jesus. It is impossible for the real Paul to sin because God has proclaimed him righteous.

Righteous men do righteous deeds. Everything you do is righteous because you are righteous. Sinful men sin because they are sinners. They did not become sinful when they sinned; they were born sinners. Their sinful acts are merely a manifestation of who they are. When you are born-again, you are born righteous. Your righteous actions are merely manifestations of your righteousness. Your righteousness taints your deeds in the same way that a man's sinful nature taints all he does. That is why people need not to worry about changing their friends when they are born-again. If they are truly born-again, many of their friendships will change. Their righteousness begins to bother their old friends.

A new believer does not even understand what is happening. The righteousness of God has been poured out into him. The justification process occurred, and that person is now righteous. His righteousness bothers the unrighteousness in the lives of his old friends even without him saying anything. He does not have to preach to his friends to cause them to shun him; his very presence convicts them. There is something in him that bothers them. He has been justified and he is now righteous.

Even though our works can never justify us, they do prove our faith and attest to the fact that we have been justified. In his letter to the church, James addresses this issue of our works validating our faith. The premise he sets forth is that true faith always manifests in action. In the same way that true love demands expression, true faith demands expression.

"Show me your faith without your works and I will show you my faith by my works . . . Was not Abraham our father justified by works when he offered Isaac his son on the altar? Do you see that faith was working together with his works and by works faith was made perfect? And the Scripture was fulfilled which says, 'Abraham believed God and it was accounted to him for righteousness.' And he was called the friend of God. You see then that a man is justified by works and not by faith only. . . For as the body without the spirit is dead, so faith with-out works is dead also" (James 2:18-26).

James is not trying to say that we are justified by our works. He is saying that faith that is not strong enough to change the way we live is not true faith. Faith is fully entrusting our lives to Him. When we do that, our lives change. It is one thing to say that you believe that you can lay hands on the sick and they recover. It is a totally different thing to actually do it. If you are not willing to lay hands on the sick and put that faith to the test, then you do not really have faith. You are just trying to convince yourself.

Abraham was justified by his work because his work was proof of his faith. He knew God would fulfill His promise even if He had to raise Isaac from the dead. His work was simply proof of his faith. Your faith must produce action, or it is not truly faith.

## SANCTIFICATION

The next aspect of the process of empowerment is sanctification. To sanctify commonly means to make holy. That is, to separate from the world and consecrate to God. The word "sanctify" is not used in the Old Testament at all and is only used ten times in the New Testament. In other places, the root words from which sanctification comes are translated "holy," "hallow," "hallowed," "holiness," "consecrate," and "saint." When Paul says that we are "saints by calling", the word he uses there is "sanctified ones." Think of sanctification as "called saints." It is important to note here, that it is not called to be saints. That is what some translations say, but you will notice that the words "to be" are in italics. That means that the translators have added those words. In Paul's first letter to the church at Corinth, he addresses the believers as those who are called saints. This word translated "called" means appointed. We have been appointed saints by God Himself. Sanctification is the process wherein we are separated from the world and consecrated to God as His holy ones.

The technical definition of sanctify means: to make holy, i.e. ceremonially purify or set apart; to venerate mentally. Although we use this word holy with great frequency in the church, few people have any real grasp of what we mean by holy. Take just a moment and try to describe what you mean when you say "holy." The best explanation of this word that I have found comes from A. W. Tozer. He defined holy as that which is "wholly other." That which is holy is unlike anything else we know. Everything we know is tainted with corruption and is impure. God is absolutely different from anything we know. That is why all our analogies and attempts to explain the Trinity fall short.

Man has tried to illustrate the doctrine of the Trinity in many different ways over the years. One explanation is that the Trinity is like the chemical formula for water — H20. H20 can take the form of liquid, gas, or solid. H20 can be steam, water, and solid ice. But H20 can't be all three at the same time in the same environment. But God is three at the same time — all the time. That presents a problem for this analogy.

Maybe God is trying to let us know that He is far too complex for us to ever fully comprehend while we still live in this realm. He is wholly other. When people ask me to explain the Trinity, my answer is always, "No!" I cannot do it. Because our understanding is limited by the realities of time and space, we cannot understand anything that is three and one at the same time. He is not three personalities. He is three individual entities; yet He is one. He wants us to know upfront that He is "wholly other."

Sanctification is the process by which God purifies the believer so that we can become "wholly other". Sanctification is based on the sacrificial death of Christ. "Just as He chose us in Him before the foundation of the world, that we should be holy and without blame before Him in love" (Ephesians 1:4). A lot of people get hung up on predestination and election. But the Scriptures are very clear — Paul tells us that He predestined us to be conformed to the image of Christ. That part of sanctification is a done deal. You will be conformed to the image of Christ because He has predestined or predetermined it.

When God predetermines it, it is done. It should give you great comfort to know that before the foundation of the world was cast, He chose you. I have no idea how that all works for I am not God. I do not have to know. All I know is that before the foundation of the world, He predetermined that I should be holy and without blame before Him in love. He knew I could not accomplish that feat on my own, so He sanctified me.

There are two parts to sanctification; God sanctifies us and then tells us to sanctify ourselves. This duality has led to some confusing teaching over the years and these teachings often ended in a contradiction to Biblical justification. So, let us examine the two parts individually.

## God's Role In Sanctification

As we have just seen, sanctification must begin with God. It is impossible for sinful man to make himself holy. By removing our sin and giving us Christ's righteousness, He begins the process of our sanctification. The fullness of the Godhead is involved in sanctification. Jude 1 tells us that we are sanctified by the Father. Hebrews 2:11 says that Christ sanctifies us and He is not ashamed to call us brethren. And in 2 Thessalonians 2:12, Paul tells us that we are sanctified by the Spirit. We are sanctified by God the Father, God the Son, and God the Holy Spirit. He is trying to tell us that this is a complete and total sanctification.

God's plan and desire is that we be totally set apart from this world. He does not want us to look, act or smell like the world. He wants us to be totally different. By dwelling in us, He makes us "wholly other." "For God did not call us to uncleanness, but in holiness" (1 Thessalonians 4:7). His presence in us makes us different. We are the dwelling place of God. He did not justify us and set us apart for us to look, smell, and act like everyone else. That is why He tells Peter that we are a chosen generation, a royal priesthood, a holy nation -- God's own peculiar possession (1 Peter 2:9).

Because the very fullness of God dwells in us, we are not like everyone else. We may play the hypocrite and try to pretend that we are just like people in the world. But we are not. We are the habitation of God. Our tastes and desires are not like those of the world.

God's desire is that we be totally and completely different from the world. Because He is "wholly other," we become "wholly other" as He dwells in us. When we submit ourselves to Christ as our Lord and Savior, placing our full faith in Him, our spirit is sanctified. As we have discussed previously, at that moment our spirit was raised and made to sit in Christ Jesus at the right hand of the Father. Our spirit became "wholly other" at that moment.

But God is not satisfied with only sanctifying our spirit. He wants to sanctify us completely. Listen to the words of Paul's closing prayer for the church in Thessalonica. "Now may the God of peace Himself sanctify you completely; and may your whole spirit, soul and body be preserved blameless at the coming of our Lord Jesus Christ" (1 Thessalonians 5:23). He is praying that God will separate and consecrate them completely. He wants to make you completely holy. You cannot do that on your own. In humility, you accept what God has done for you. He has made you holy. He has set you apart from the world. He has separated you for Himself. Therefore He told us to work out our own salvation in fear and trembling (Philippians 4:12). He is saying, "Take what I am doing in your life - this separation - and walk in fullness. Be different - sanctified - in your mind, your will, and your emotions. Let the sanctification of your spirit walk out in your soul and body."

## Man's Role In Sanctification

We are commanded to live a holy life and to be separate from the world - this is our responsibility. He sanctified us and justified us. He made us holy and righteous. Now, he simply says, "Act like it! I made you different. Quit trying to act like the world." The amazing thing is that the church continually tries to act like the world, so that it will be more appealing to the world. But the world does not want a church that looks like the world. They already have the world.

They want the church to be different. The world does not expect the church to look like the night club. We do not understand that. When the world comes into the church, they expect something different. They do not want it to feel like the Rotary Club. They want it to be different. They want to see something unusual. They hear that this is where God shows up. But for some reason, we think that we must make it compatible with the world.

Today, we are trying to make the church more palatable to the world's ideas and comfort. This mindset is often referred to a being "seeker friendly." But a person that is truly seeking is seeking an experience with God. Heal a blind child and I guarantee you will be seeker friendly. Feed five thousand with a couple of loaves and a few little fish — that is seeker friendly. It will draw a crowd. Walk through the hospital halls and heal people — you will draw a crowd.

Jesus was terrible at salesmanship. He talked about having to die to self to follow him. He said things like "sell all you have," "let the dead bury the dead," "take up your cross," and "if you follow Me, people will hate you." Yet, He could not keep the crowds away. The world wants to see a difference. The world expects us to live differently. By our own futile attempts at salesmanship, we prove that we do not want to be too different. We think people will not want to be Christian if we are too different. But we are different — totally different.

We are so different that we live by totally different standards. We are even told to present our bodies as slaves of righteousness (Romans 6:19). We are not slaves of the law. We are not sanctified by the Law. We now have the Law written in our hearts and minds. The eternal Word of God dwells in us. That is why Romans 12:1 tells us to "present our members as slaves of righteousness. We are righteous and we need to learn to obey that righteousness that is within us. In other words, "present your members as slaves of the righteous person you are in the spirit realm." Make your members come into submission to your spirit. The righteous man that you are should rule the flesh that you dwell in. Do not let your flesh confine you. You dictate to the body what you will do.

We must put our faith in Jesus. We are sanctified by faith in Him. Paul was a Jew among Jews. He was possibly a member of the Sanhedrin and understood trying to live a sanctified life by the Law. But when He met God on the Damascus road, all of that changed. He was commissioned into a ministry that freed men from the limits and bondages of the Law. He told King Agrippa that the Lord sent him "to open their eyes, in order to turn them from darkness to light and from the power of Satan to God, that they may receive forgiveness of sins and an inheritance among those who are sanctified by faith in Christ" (Acts 26:18). Paul's ministry was a ministry of liberation from legalism.

We find the message of sanctification by faith over and over in his writings. He continually preached that we must learn to live in the Spirit, which means to live out the sanctification we have in Christ. When we live our lives focused on who we are in Christ and how set apart we are, we put to death the evil deeds of the flesh. We do not put these deeds to death by focusing on them and making rules and laws against them. That is living by the flesh or living by the law. Only by living by the Spirit (focusing upon our sanctification by faith) can we enter into the fullness of life. "For if you live according to the flesh you will die; but if by the Spirit you put to death the deeds of the body, you will live" (Romans 8:13). It seems that every time the subject of holiness surfaces in the church, people tend to get off into legalism. They begin to live, not according to the spirit, but according to the law. But you can never sanctify yourself with rules and regulations. The more you try, the harder you fail.

For instance, suppose I were to tell you that I had determined to begin loving more. I made up a list of rules that made me perform certain acts that people who love to perform. The list called for me to give a certain portion of my money to the poor every week, to help one elderly person every day, to play with one orphan every week, and visit one sick person every day. Doing those things would not make me love more. Love must come from the heart. But if I love, I will do these types of things without thinking about it.

We could take the issue of self-control as another example. If I control Self with my Self, Self wins. That is what Paul addresses in the last few verses of Colossians 2.

> "Therefore, if you died with Christ from the basic principles of the world, why, as though living in the world,

do you subject yourselves to regulations — "Do not touch, do not taste, do not handle," which all concern things which perish with the using — according to the commandments and doctrines of men? These things indeed have an appearance of wisdom in self-imposed religion, false humility, and neglect of the body, but are of no value against the indulgence of the flesh."

You can never sanctify yourself with rules and regulations. You sanctify yourself by walking in the Spirit. If you try to control the urges of the flesh with self-control, Self wins. If you control the flesh with the flesh, the flesh wins.

When you walk in the Spirit, the flesh is removed, and the fruit of the Spirit begins to appear. When we walk in the Spirit, we begin to notice a change in our heart and behavior. The fruit of the Spirit is that which is produced in us as we put our faith in and focus on the set-apart nature we have in Christ. There is no law or set of regulations that will produce the fruit of the spirit. "But the fruit of the spirit is love, joy, peace, long-suffering, kindness, goodness, faithfulness, gentleness, self-control. Against such there is no law. And those who are Christ's have crucified the flesh with its passions and desires" (Galatians 5:22-24). The Fruit of the Spirit is the fruit produced in us as His Spirit flows through us. Our responsibility is to keep our eyes focused on who we are in Christ and how he has sanctified us until those fruits are produced in our life. He has set us apart as his own special people. We are "wholly other" in our very nature. Because we are sanctified, we live a "set-apart" live. This sanctified living causes us to walk in the glory He has given us.

## GLORIFICATION

In that process of walking in the spirit, we discover the glory that has been given to us. In the Garden of Gethsemane, Jesus said that the glory God had given to Him, He has given to us. The word translated glory or glorified is the Greek word *doxodzo*. We get the English word doxology directly from this word. It means to render (or esteem) glorious; to magnify; to honor. The honor and glory in which Jesus walked, is the honor and glory He has given to us and expects us to walk therein. So, one must wonder about this glory that was given to Him. According to John 1:14 that glory is sonship. "And the Word became flesh and dwelt among us, and we beheld His glory, the glory as of the only begotten of the Father, full of grace and truth." He has glorified us as sons of God. We have the same glorious relationship with the Father as Christ for we are in Him, and He is in us.

In Paul's famous assurance passage at the end of Romans 8, he says, "whom He called, these He also justified; and whom He justified, these He also glorified." Most Christians believe that God is going to glorify us some day. Most believe that one day we will die, receive our glorified bodies, and go to heaven. But notice the tense of this word. It does not say that God is going to glorify us. It says that He has glorified us. This event has already occurred. We must come to the place where we comprehend and accept the fact that God has given us the glory. We want to glorify God, but He wants to glorify us. He glorifies us by doing his work in us and through us. We are His children. He receives glory when we receive glory.

Again, in that famous eighth chapter of Romans, Paul says, "For I consider that the sufferings of this present time are not worthy to be compared with the glory which shall be revealed in us." He is not just talking about when we die. He is talking about the sons of God walking in the revelation of who we are in Christ. As we grow in this revelation, we grow in the glorification that accompanies that walk. It is the principle that Peter was talking about in 2 Peter 1:4, when he says that through the precious promises of God, we become "partakers of the divine nature." We move into oneness with Christ and the glory given to us is revealed.

In humility, we understand that apart from Christ we are nothing, but in Christ we can do all things. Over and over the Scriptures tell us that God exalts the humble and brings down the proud. God tells us that if we will humble ourselves and allow Him to work in us and through us, then He will exalt us. If we try to exalt ourselves by living our own way, by living by the Law, He will bring us down. It is only in our humility that we can allow Christ to sanctify us and walk in that sanctification. This is what Paul is addressing when he says, "I live yet not I but Christ lives in me" (Galatians 2:20). When we live in that manner, we live in the glory of God.

Our glory is in what God has made us and in what God is doing through us. In the Garden of Gethsemane, Jesus prayed, "And all Mine are Yours and Yours are Mine and I am glorified in them" (John 17:10). Christ is glorified when we allow Him to empower us through justification, sanctification, and glorification. When we allow the fullness of the Godhead to operate in us and through us, we touch the world around us with the presence and power of God. When we do this, we bring God glory. We bring God glory by humbling ourselves and allowing Him to do good things for us. We bring God glory when, in humility, we say, "Lord Jesus, I need these things to accomplish your will. I expect these things because You have promised." Every good and perfect gift comes down from the Father above. When we allow Him to pour His gifts out on us, we bring Him glory.

He has justified us so that we are worthy to receive His empowerment. He has set us apart to walk in that empowerment. He has glorified us with His empowerment and this empowerment brings Him glory. The world is yet to see what can happen when God's children walk in His empowerment and glory ... but it can begin in you right now.

This series is currently available in English, French and Nepali. For information about securing copies please contact one of the following:

## USA
**CITIPOINTE CHURCH**
307 N. First St.
Wylie, TX 75098
972.422.9111
pastor@citipointe.org

## AFRICA

### French Translation
Rev James Wheagar
San Pedro, Cote D'voire
Eglise.mevac@gmail.com
+225-07329768

### English Translation
Bishop Paul Yesani
newmannai@yahoo.com
Lilongwe, Malawi

Pastor George Ngayaye
Johannesburg, South Africa
27 79 243 4717

Made in the USA
Middletown, DE
15 October 2023